Texans in the
Confederate Cavalry

CIVIL WAR CAMPAIGNS AND COMMANDERS SERIES

Under the General Editorship of Grady McWhiney

PUBLISHED

Battle in the Wilderness: Grant Meets Lee by Grady McWhiney
Death in September: The Antietam Campaign
        by Perry D. Jamieson
Texans in the Confederate Cavalry by Anne J. Bailey
Sam Bell Maxey and the Confederate Indians by John C. Waugh

FORTHCOMING

General James Longstreet in the West: A Monumental Failure
        by Judith Lee Hallock
The Saltville Massacre by Tom Mays
Battle of the Crater by Jeff Kinard
The Dahlgren Raid by David Long

Texans in the
Confederate Cavalry

Anne J. Bailey

Under the General Editorship of Grady McWhiney

MCWHINEY
FOUNDATION
PRESS

MCMURRY UNIVERSITY
ABILENE, TEXAS

Cataloging-in-Publication Data

Bailey, Anne J.
    Texans in the Confederate Cavalry/ Anne J. Bailey
        p. cm. — (Civil War campaigns and commanders)
    Includes bibliographical references and index.
    ISBN 1-886661-02-2 (pbk.)

    1. Confederate States of America. Army. Texas Cavalry.
2. United States—History—Civil War, 1861–1865—Cavalry operations.
3. Confederate States of America. Army. Texas Cavalry. 4. Texas—
History—Civil War, 1861–1865—Cavalry operations. I. Title.
II. Series.
    E546.5.B347 1995
    973.7'464'0922—dc20   95–11704
                                                  CIP

McMurry Station, Box 637
Abilene, TX 79697-0637

Printed in the United States of America

ISBN 1-886661-02-2

10 9 8 7 6 5 4 3 2 1

Book Designed by Rosenbohm Design Group

All inquiries regarding volume purchases of this book should be addressed to
MCWHINEY FOUNDATION PRESS, McMurry Station, Box 637, Abilene, TX 79697-0637.
Telephone inquiries may be made by calling (915) 691-6681.

A Note on the Series

Few segments of America's past excite more interest than Civil War battles and leaders. This ongoing series of brief, lively, and authoritative books–*Civil War Campaigns and Commanders*–salutes this passion with inexpensive and accurate accounts that are readable in a sitting. Each volume, separate and complete in itself, nevertheless conveys the agony, glory, death, and wreckage that defined America's greatest tragedy.

In this series, designed for Civil War enthusiasts as well as the newly recruited, emphasis is on telling good stories. Photographs and biographical sketches enhance the narrative of each book, and maps depict events as they happened. Sound history is meshed with the dramatic in a format that is just lengthy enough to inform and yet satisfy.

Grady McWhiney
General Editor

CONTENTS

CAMPAIGNS AND COMMANDERS SERIES

Map Key

Geography

Trees

Marsh

Fields

Strategic Elevations

Rivers

Tactical Elevations

)(Fords

Orchards

——·—— Political Boundaries

Human Construction

Bridges

+++++++ Railroads

Tactical Towns

• Strategic Towns

■ Buildings

‡ Church

⤬ Roads

Military

Union Infantry

Confederate Infantry

Cavalry

ıḷı Artillery

Headquarters

△ △△
△ △△ Encampments
△ △△
△ △ △

Fortifications

Permanant Works

Hasty Works

Obstructions

✗ Engagements

Warships

Gunboats

Casemate Ironclad

Monitor

Tactical Movements

Strategic Movements

Maps by
Donald S. Frazier, PhD.
Abilene, Texas

MAPS

PHOTOGRAPHS

The brief biographies accompanying the photographs were written
by Grady McWhiney and David Coffey.

Texans in the Confederate Cavalry

1

Mounted Texans Go to War

Stretching over 800 miles from north to south and almost that far from east to west, Texas was the largest of the Confederate states. Covering more than 266,000 square miles, the area equaled all of Virginia (including West Virginia), North Carolina, South Carolina, Georgia, and Alabama combined. An active Indian frontier discouraged some prospective settlers, but an increase of 184.2 percent in the decade before the Civil War propelled the population to over 604,000. Less than 5 percent of the people lived in towns, and the frontier atmosphere found in the urban areas provided a colorful contrast to the elegance of many Southern cities. British traveler Colonel Arthur J.L. Fremantle, who found Texans "very agreeable", believed their good nature developed "in spite of their peculiar habits of hanging, shooting, &c., which seemed to be natural to people living in a wild and thinly-populated country." When the Civil War came, Texans often claimed that their affinity for fighting had roots on the state's frontier.

Even before Texas voted to leave the Union early in March 1861, men rushed to join military companies. One anxious Texan feared "the grand, decisive battle would be fought" before he could reach the "seat of active operations." J.T. Hunter recounted: "I well remember how great was the excitement in my old town of Huntsville and how often at night youths, students from the college, stood on the courthouse steps and harangued the people, inciting them to greater enthusiasm and desire to go to the front." Hunter eventually joined the infantry, serving in Hood's Texas Brigade in the Army of Northern Virginia. Another anxious recruit, D.H. Combs, recalled: "I was very fearful the war would be over before I saw a live Yankee. So Charley McGehee and I went fifty miles from home to join a company." These two friends became members of the 8th Texas Cavalry, better known as Terry's Texas Rangers.

Texans volunteered so enthusiastically that by late March the first cavalry regiment mustered into the Confederate Army, followed by over thirty more cavalry regiments, and numerous miscellaneous battalions, mounted state troops, and independent companies.

There was a singularity about the Texas soldier. Victor M. Rose, who belonged to the 3rd Texas Cavalry, noted that the companies had names such as "Texas Hunters" and "Dead-Shot Rangers." After the war a trooper recalled: "To us, Texas was the 'nation'; to her alone we owed allegiance. We were *allied* with the other Southern States, not indissolubly *joined.*"

Throughout the war, Texas contributed more cavalry regiments to the Confederacy than any other state. But most Texans served in the Trans-Mississippi theater, and never

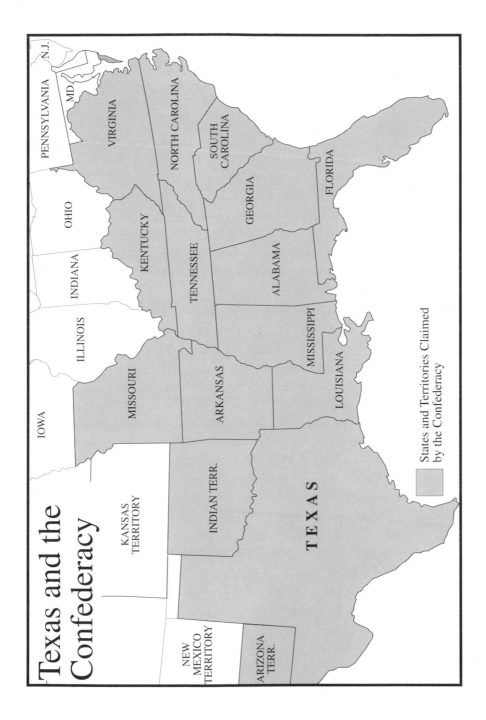

Texas and the Confederacy

States and Territories Claimed by the Confederacy

received the recognition given to units serving east of the Mississippi River. No Texas cavalry regiments rode with the Army of Northern Virginia, and only a handful served in the Western theater. Even so, Texans proudly claimed their own full Confederate general, Albert Sidney Johnston, and one lieutenant general, John Bell Hood; both had belonged to the 2d U.S. Cavalry, a regiment stationed in Texas prior to the war. But these two men led armies far from the Lone Star State while the majority of Texans in the Confederate cavalry served in Arkansas, Louisiana, and Indian Territory. Approximately half of the numbered Texas cavalry regiments fought in the Trans-Mississippi. Over one-third were ultimately dismounted, while the rest saw action in Tennessee, Mississippi, Georgia, and the Carolinas. Government records indicate that Texas cavalry utilized the regimental designations 1st through 37th, although many units were known by different names, and duplication sometimes occurred. Those who saw the most fighting served in units east of the Mississippi where they operated primarily as scouts and raiders.

At the war's outbreak, Texas had little problem raising cavalry. Oran M. Roberts, who later commanded the 11th Texas Infantry, recalled: "Almost any one who could get authority from the general or from the secretary of war could raise battalions or regiments of cavalry. It became obvious that if any considerable number of infantry were raised in a reasonable time, that men of personal influence with the people must undertake it. Even then it was necessary to raise infantry troops for twelve months' service."

Governor Edward Clark observed in November 1861 that the Texans' desire to join the cavalry was founded "upon their peerless horsemanship." They were "unwilling in many instances to engage in service of any other description, unless required by actual necessity. This passion for mounted service is manifest in the fact that no call for cavalry has yet been made which has not been complied with almost instantaneously, and there are companies of this character now throughout the State which are eager for service."

By December the cavalry leaving the state outnumbered the infantry by nearly two and a half to one—over 17,000 cavalrymen to around 7,100 infantrymen. This disparity continued to escalate in spite of the state government's efforts to recruit infantry. By mid-1862 Texas cavalrymen numbered

Oran Milo Roberts: born South Carolina 1815; graduated from University of Alabama in 1836; studied law and was admitted to the bar in 1837; served a term in the Alabama Legislature; in 1841 moved to San Augustine, Texas, to practice law; appointed district attorney in 1844; district judge from 1846 to 1851; became president of the board of trustees and lecturer in law at University of San Augustine in 1845; associate justice of the Texas Supreme Court in 1857; a strong secessionist, he was unanimously elected president of the state Secession Convention in 1861; raised the 11th Texas Infantry and served as its colonel; in November 1863, while with Brigadier General Tom Green in Louisiana, led an attack on Federals at Bayou Bourbeau; Roberts reported: "Our whole line responded at once and rushed towards the enemy, and continued it through the enemy's camp, they having fled before us." In 1864, Roberts left the army to become chief justice of the Texas Supreme Court; removed from office when the war ended, he served as a member of the Constitutional Convention of 1866; elected by the Texas Legislature to the U. S. Senate, but was denied his seat because of his Confederate activities; with the restoration of Democratic  control in Texas, he returned to the Supreme Court until elected governor of Texas in 1878; upon his retirement in 1883, he became professor of law at the University of Texas; wrote several books and contributed to Dudley G. Wooten's *Comprehensive History of Texas* (1898) and Clement A. Evans' *Confederate Military History*, XI (1898). Roberts died in Austin in 1898.

approximately 28,500—an estimated 7,800 Texans served on the east side of the Mississippi, about 7,400 in Arkansas, and some 13,300 more were en route to Little Rock. This number is impressive. The 1860 census indicated that Texas has 92,145 white males between the ages of eighteen and forty-five, so these cavalrymen represented nearly a third of the state's military population—and surely an even higher proportion if those incapable of serving for one reason or another were deleted from the total eligible.

Edward Clark: born Georgia 1815; his father, John Clark, served as governor; left Georgia after his father's death in 1832, and moved to Montgomery, Alabama,

where he studied, then practiced, law; in 1842, he relocated to Marshall, Texas, and three years later was a member of the Convention of 1845 which approved the annexation of the Republic of Texas to the United States; served in the first Texas House of Representatives, and a senator in the Second Legislature; as a member of the staff of General James Pinckney Henderson during the Mexican War, Clark fought in the Battle of Monterrey; in the 1850s, he served as secretary of state under Governor Elisha M. Pease, and was elected lieutenant governor in 1859, running on an independent ticket with Sam Houston; when Houston refused to take an oath of allegiance to the Confederacy in 1861, the Texas Secession Convention declared Clark the governor; he took the oath of office in March, and completed Houston's term; defeated for re-election by Francis R. Lubbock, Clark raised the 14th Texas Infantry and became its colonel; fought in the Red River Campaign, and was wounded at the Battle of Mansfield while leading his regiment in a charge; on the next day at Pleasant Hill, Clark was shot through the leg just under the knee, disabling him for further service; fled to Mexico after the war, but soon returned to Texas, settling eventually in Marshall where he practiced law. He died there in 1880. Clark "is remembered as one of the best of the fighting governors of Texas."

Convincing Texans to become foot soldiers proved difficult. Perhaps Texan John Wesley Rabb, a member of the 8th Texas Cavalry, phrased it best when he wrote his mother from Chattanooga, Tennessee, in June 1862: "I wood rather be corporal in company F of the Texas Rangers than to be first Lieu[tenant] in a flat foot company." The Englishman Colonel Fremantle noted the partiality of Texans for the cavalry: "At the outbreak of the war it was found very difficult to raise infantry in Texas, as no Texan walks a yard if he can help it."

Nevertheless, some cavalry units had trouble filling their quotas until after the passage of the Conscription Act in April 1862, when many Texans hastily joined a cavalry unit to avoid conscription into the infantry, a prospect few of them relished. This partially accounts for the increase in cavalrymen in the period between December 1861 and June 1862, when the number quickly swelled by 11,500. This prompted Governor Francis R. Lubbock to advise Secretary of War Judah P. Benjamin in March 1862 that in spite of repeated protests from the state government too many Texans were still being given permission from Richmond to raise cavalry. He believed that allowing them to do so defeated "every effort I can make to raise infantry. If cavalry is wanted I could fill your requisition in twenty days."

The solution reached was unpopular; Texas raised the cavalrymen and Richmond dismounted them. "You know," explained Private Frank M. Files, "it was almost impossible to get a Texan to join the infantry." The method used by the Confederate government "was to organize a cavalry troop and then dismount them," though the boys "sure did kick when they found they had been tricked." A Pennsylvania-born chaplain of the 8th Texas Cavalry wrote in 1863 that it was "a burning shame that such horsemen as Texians are, and I may justly add, such fighters, too, should be put in the infantry service." He was appalled that men from other states, "poorly mounted, poorly armed and shamefully poor horsemen," had become cavalry. He considered them "a reproach to this honorable arm of the service, and...a loss to the web foots

Francis Richard Lubbock: born South Carolina 1815; educated in private schools until his father died, but at age fourteen had to go to work as a hardware clerk in Charleston; managed a cotton warehouse in Hamburg, South Carolina, before moving in 1834 to New Orleans and opening a drug store; in 1836 relocated to Houston, Texas, where he claimed to have sold the first barrel of flour for $30 and the first sack of coffee for twenty-five cents a pound; served as clerk of the Texas House of Representatives of the Second Congress; at the age of twenty-two appointed comptroller of the Republic by Sam Houston; in 1840 reentered

mercantile business in Houston and the next year elected district clerk of Harris County; in 1846 bought a four hundred acre ranch south of Houston; helped organize the Democratic party in Texas in 1856; elected lieutenant governor the following year; as a delegate to the Democratic National Convention at Charleston in 1860, Lubbock supported the Jefferson Davis faction and later favored secession; elected governor over Edward Clark in 1861, Lubbock took office with the treasury empty, Texas bonds not selling, and the Indians hostile; he cooperated with the Confederacy; established cloth and shoe manufacturing at the state penitentiary; and persuaded the legislature to raise a regiment of cavalry for frontier defense, establish cotton trade through Mexico, and manufacture war materials for state troops; he retired voluntarily from the governorship in 1863; served on the staff of Major General John B. Magruder and later with Major General John A. Wharton; in 1864 Lubbock became aide to President Jefferson Davis, acting chiefly as advisor on Trans-Mississippi affairs; captured with Davis in 1865 and imprisoned for several months; after being released, he returned to Texas and re-entered business, losing heavily in a beef-packing venture; served three years as tax collector of Galveston and was then elected state treasurer in 1878 and for five additional terms; served the James S. Hogg administration as a member of the board of pardons, retiring finally from public service at the age of eighty; published *Six Decades in Texas* (1900) and died in Austin in 1905.

where they [belonged, and where they] would be compelled to do good fighting."

Texans encouraged the impression that they were superior horsemen and better equipped for mounted service than the average soldier. They were quick to point out that Texas Rangers had patrolled the rolling hills and windswept plains west of San Antonio since the days of the Republic. Although only a handful of the men who became Confederate soldiers had ever fought an Indian, Texas' military heritage, born in a revolution against Mexico in the 1830s and maturing in the Mexican-American War of the 1840s, touched all who lived there. Usually the Texan made an excellent mounted soldier, and this military tradition served him well. At other times this frontier background only served to make him too independent for the rank and file.

2

THE LONE STAR CAVALRYMAN

"At the beginning of the war," recalled R.M. Collins, "young Texans in the saddle was regarded as a whole set put together in thirds; one-third man and bell spurs, one-third gun, pistol and knife, and one-third pony." Image meant almost as much to the Texan as his desire to become a valued soldier. With the proper attitude and attire, the Texan felt he could intimidate Yankees into surrendering. While it was true that most of those men who enrolled early in the war had never ridden the West Texas frontier, they believed they had a reputation to uphold, for tales of Davy Crockett and the Alamo had already become the seeds of legend. This superficial, even naive, view of a cavalryman's role meant that the Texas soldier often caused as much trouble for his own officers as he did for the enemy's. Both inexperienced and impressionable, recruits thought that the war would give them a chance to prove they were worthy of the name "Texian."

The men who joined in 1861 were young, and mostly unmarried. In the 12th Texas Cavalry, organized in the summer of 1861, 85 percent of the privates were in their twenties or younger. Only about 11 percent were in their thirties, and less than 4 percent over forty. One year later, however, the average age for men joining a similar regiment was higher; both privates and officers tended to be around three years older. In fact, probably because of the conscription law, the number of enlistees in their thirties was two and one-third times as great as in 1861 while the number of teenagers declined. Even after passage of the law, 10 percent of the recruits still exceeded the age of thirty-five, at which point they were exempt. Those men over the draft age chose to enlist for a variety of reasons, but in Texas, where the environment helped mold the man, remaining at home became unacceptable.

Regardless of the reason for volunteering, the rush of patriotism in 1861 or the threat of the draft in 1862, enlisting was an informal process. In a frontier county south of Dallas a newly appointed captain appealed to the citizens' sense of loyalty while he provided them with free whiskey. At the proper time he mounted a big box he had placed in the center of the square and called for volunteers. "All that... [want] to go away in my company just form a line right out in front of me," he shouted. Nearly fifty citizens, spirits stimulated by the free drinks, came forward. "Now gentlemen," the captain stated, "raise your right hands, pull off your hats and I will now administer the oath to you and muster you into the service." Men lined up next to their friends, the liquor continued to flow, and the next morning many awoke to discover they had joined the "Johnson County Slashers."

After enlistment liquor continued to cause trouble. In October 1861 a member of the 8th Texas Cavalry wrote from Kentucky: "Whisky is very hard to get in camp as it is strickly forbiden to be sole in Bolin Green to Solgers, and we are forbiden to bring it in to camp, but we Bucks alwayes have a suply on hand." The regiment's commander placed guards

Samuel J. Richardson: born Virginia 1825; settled in Marshall, Texas, with his mother, a wealthy widow, who taught her son early to take responsibility; when his mother objected to a railroad laying track in front of her home, Sam waited for the builders to reach her property before he "took a stand there with a shotgun and said he would kill the first man who stuck a pick or shovel on that line"; the track passed further to the north; equally dedicated to the South, he belonged to the radical Knights of the Golden Circle, a secret, prewar, pro-Southern organization; early in 1860 he had visited New Orleans to discuss the status of the KGC in Texas and possibly finalize plans for an invasion of Mexico, but their hopes for establishing a protectorate over Mexico ended as the problems within the Union

Capt. Sam. J. Richardson.

intensified; Richardson therefore turned his attention to the preservation of states' rights; tax records indicate that he and his mother jointly held nine slaves and some cattle for a net worth of $17,000 in 1861; Richardson raised a company called the W.P. Lane Rangers after a leading citizen of Marshall; the Rangers joined the 2d Texas Cavalry, commanded by Colonel John S. Ford, and served on the Texas frontier the first year of the war; Richardson made numerous pleas and at least two trips to Richmond before obtaining permission for his company to become an independent command; he persuaded ninety out of a hundred of his men to rejoin at the reorganization of the Confederate armies in the spring of 1862; then, recalled a soldier, "the boys all went to town to pledge their fidelity to each other and their country; by getting on a big spree"; after moving his company north to reinforce other Confederates defending Fort Hindman at Arkansas Post, Richardson and about half his men were captured when the post surrendered in January 1863; after being exchanged, Richardson joined the remnants of his command and spent most of 1863 scouting and guarding Federal prisoners in East Texas; in 1864 the company officially joined Charles L. Morgan's Regiment, a hodgepodge of independent companies, in Colonel William Henry Parsons' Cavalry Brigade.

around the camps to prevent the men from going into town, but a trooper recalled that the boys "looked upon this as an unnecessary restriction upon their general liberty, and so some of the most determined ones would manage to get out and go up every night and sometimes they would get unruly or noisy from drink and fall into the hands of the police and be locked up; but generally they were released after short detention and a promise of good behavior in the future."

The Texan's ability to consume considerable amounts of alcohol provided a constant source of amazement to visitors. Colonel Fremantle commented that while journeying through Texas in 1863 he became "comparatively accustomed and reconciled to the necessity of shaking hands and drinking brandy with every one." Moreover, Fremantle, who visited every Confederate state except Arkansas and Florida, claimed: "This necessity does not exist [anywhere] except in Texas." Yet he admitted: "There was much to like in my fellow-travellers. They all had a sort of *bonhommie* honesty and straight-forwardness, a natural courtesy and extreme good-nature, which was very agreeable." Texas Rangers, observed Fremantle, "were very picturesque fellows; tall, thin, and ragged, but quite gentlemanlike in their manners."

While most Texans were friendly and outgoing, they could also become rowdy and unmanageable. Private James J. Frazier warned his family not to believe everything that appeared in the newspapers, and particularly not to worry that he was involved in anything improper. After some lively recruits, filled with too much whiskey, celebrated their induction into the Confederate army, a much exaggerated account of their arrest appeared in the local press. Frazier anxiously assured his family that it was only an isolated incident. "Some of the boys got drunk," he explained in a letter home, "and run thrugh town firing off pistols & broke into a grocery story and took the man's whiskey & done other things unbecuming to a sivalized soldier." On another occasion in

Galveston a half-drunken cavalryman from the 2d Texas Mounted Rifles tried to halt a wagon by aiming his six-shooter at the driver. When the man refused to stop, the Texan fired five shots at him, the last killing one of the horses. A captain from Louisiana, apparently not fond of Texans, claimed that the soldier's regiment would probably hang him—not for attempting to shoot the wagon driver, but for being such a "disgraceful bad shot" and missing.

Texans did nothing to discourage this rough-and-tumble frontier image; indeed, they often tried to embellish it. A private in the 21st Texas Cavalry proudly boasted in 1862 that the Federals seemed "afraid even to send out scouts, for fear that we will bush-whack them." Such audacity only served to promote the Texans' rapidly spreading reputation of invincibility, and citizens often believed Texans could frighten Yankees out of a region simply by their presence. A soldier in Arkansas told his wife, "as we were charging and fighting along the road the ladies would run out into the road and cheer us and wave their pocket handkerchiefs" shouting "huza for the Texas rangers; huza for the Texas rangers."

Convinced they had an image to uphold, Texans became aggressive fighters. Victor Rose of the 3rd Texas Cavalry recalled that the Texas soldier had great confidence in "his own prowess." They loved a glorious charge, gaining a reputation for fearless, often brutal fighting on both sides of the Mississippi River. A newspaper reported that the Yankees "have a great deal more fear of Texas Rangers than they have of the devil." The July 1861 edition of *Harper's Weekly* carried a harrowing description of a Texas cavalryman, along with a sketch of a fierce looking man under a huge Mexican sombrero with long hair and a bushy beard and mustache. The caption portrayed the Texas Ranger as a "desperate" fellow, "mounted on a mustang horse...[and] armed with a pair of Colt navy revolvers, a rifle, a tomahawk, a Texan bowie-knife, and a lasso. They are described as being very dexterous in the use of the latter." *Harper's*, however, failed to mention spurs, an essential item to any Texas cavalryman's attire. A visitor to a camp of instruction near Houston observed that many of the men had "the appearance of fierce warriors" who wore huge "bell-spurs" on their boots and had vicious looking knives dangling around their waists. In fact, Colonel Fremantle noted, "These Rangers all wear the most enormous spurs I ever saw." Throughout the war these spurs remained a Texas trademark. On Sherman's flank in the Carolinas just before the war's end, a company of Confederate scouts challenged some mounted Texans who had accompanied General Joseph Wheeler across the Pee Dee River. The scouts insisted that only Yankees were in the vicinity; therefore, the mounted men could not be Texans. Texan E.H. McKnight recalled: "I had a hard time to make the captain understand that General Wheeler was at the house, for he said he left Wheeler on the other side of the river; but I finally showed him that I was a Texan Ranger by my boots and Texas spurs."

Four years of fighting had only increased the Texan's distinctiveness, and those forty-eight months of war had also reinforced his reputation as a fighter. Being a Texas cavalryman required more than riding a horse well; it demanded a certain flair, a style representative of the frontier traditions of the Lone Star state. Boots, bell spurs, or a simple silver star pinned to a hat were all Texas trademarks, objects the soldier used to emphasize his singularity. He gave little thought to what it meant to be a professional soldier, particularly if it required relinquishing any of his identity. A Texas Ranger would scoff at the notion that he needed book learning to survive, and he refused to surrender any of his independence in order to achieve military propriety. As a result, Texans might annoy and exasperate their officers, but they seldom failed when it came time to act.

3

THE INDEPENDENT
TEXAS TROOPER

The cavalry was not for everyone, for it could prove expensive to secure the proper paraphernalia. While the foot soldier often left for war with only a musket or rifle, the cavalryman needed a horse and equipment. Having the wherewithal to acquire a mount frequently gave the horseman a sense of superiority, as riding provided a freedom of movement that his comrades in the infantry did not enjoy. The Texan often stretched the liberties allowed a trooper to the limits, and frequently tested the patience of his officers. Yet this freedom only extended as far as his mount could carry him, and the trooper's greatest fear was the loss of his horse.

Survival meant a sturdy horse, and Confederate cavalrymen generally furnished their own, along with everything else they needed. The price of a Texas steed in

1861 was about $135 for a private and $156 for an officer. Should an animal be disabled or killed, its owner had to replace it quickly or be transferred to the infantry, a humiliation to most Texans. In May 1862 a Texan wrote home: "Horses bear tremendous prices," as the company's lieutenant

Benjamin Franklin Terry: born Kentucky 1821; moved with his mother and brothers to Brazoria County, Texas, in 1831; married Mary Bingham, daughter of one of Stephen F. Austin's "Old Three Hundred," in 1841; engaged in sugar cane planting in Fort Bend County during the 1850s; one of the state's wealthiest men, owning over 100 slaves; served as a delegate to the Texas Secession Convention in 1861; after the convention adjourned, Frank went to Virginia with John A. Wharton and Thomas S. Lubbock; participated in the First Battle of Manassas on the staff of Brigadier General James Longstreet who reported: "Cols. B.F. Terry and T. Lubbock were very active and energetic. When unoccupied, they repeatedly volunteered their services to make reconnaissances," and at Fairfax Courthouse, "Colonel Terry, with his unerring rifle, severed the halliard and thus lowered the Federal flag found still floating from the cupola of the courthouse there." Terry returned to Houston, and organized a regiment, the 8th Texas Cavalry, known as Terry's Texas Rangers, which joined Albert Sidney

Johnston's army in Kentucky; Terry died leading a charge against Federal forces at the Battle of Woodsonville, Kentucky, on December 17, 1861; a Union colonel reported: "With lightning speed, under infernal yelling, great numbers of Texas Rangers rushed upon our whole force. They advanced as near as 15 or 20 yards to our lines, some of them even between them, and then opened fire with rifles and shotguns." A Texan recalled: "Terry ordered a charge, when our boys raised a shout …they dashed right into them and began shooting and the Yankees began to run." Terry died instantly, just a few miles from his birthplace. "We had other brave leaders," wrote one cavalryman, "but none like the matchless Terry." Over six feet tall, with broad shoulders, and a large brow and blond whiskers, he was said to resemble "one of the Norsemen who came over with Leif Ericson."

had sold his for $300. In November 1862 a cavalryman in Arkansas informed his wife: "Dont sell off any more horses unless it is to supply yourself with the necessaries of life. Horses are worth twice as much now as a year ago and if the war continues they will be higher still." Six months later, in June 1863, inflation prompted a Trans-Mississippi trooper to

James Knox Polk Blackburn: born Tennessee 1837; moved with his family to Texas in 1856, and studied for two years at Alma Institute in Lavaca County, Texas; teaching school when secession crisis began, Blackburn joined the force commanded by Ben McCulloch that accepted the surrender of Federal troops at San Antonio; enlisted in a company that became part of the 8th Texas Cavalry

(Terry's Texas Rangers); the regiment left Houston in September and traveled by railroad, boat, foot, and cart to New Orleans, where its commander received an invitation to join General Albert Sidney Johnston's army in Kentucky; first engagement in December 1861 at Woodsonville, Kentucky; Blackburn fought at the Battle of Shiloh in April 1862; elected first lieutenant a few weeks later and shortly thereafter he became captain; served with his unit in all major engagements until seriously wounded in both legs during the Battle of Farmington, Tennessee, in October 1863; he refused to allow the amputation of his legs, and was captured by Federal forces; paroled for hospitalization, he recuperated in Tennessee but was unable to return to duty with the Rangers until February 1865; saw no further action because his exchange was not validated until the surrender of Joseph E. Johnston's army in April 1865; after the war, he settled in Giles County, Tennessee, married, and became a large land owner; served for a time in the Tennessee legislature. Before his death in 1923, he published "Reminiscences of the Terry Rangers," *Southwestern Historical Quarterly*, XXII (1918) in which he wrote: "I wear four scars on my body from Yankee bullets that will go with me to my grave, but I regard them as scars of honor received in defense of the Southland, and am proud of them."

observe: "Horses here transcend all bounds, rating from $25 to $800." R.L. Dunman, who served east of the river with the Army of Tennessee, recalled: "It was a cavalryman's business to keep mounted, and we had to be a pretty resourceful bunch of young fellows to do this. If our horses were shot from under us, we usually 'managed' to get another one! As a cavalryman I was never compelled to walk but *one* day during the entire war!"

The 8th Texas Cavalry, a regiment raised by Benjamin Franklin Terry, and later known as Terry's Texas Rangers, became mounted under unusual circumstances. The men left Texas on foot, planning to find horses when they arrived in Virginia. But they never made it that far. General Albert Sidney Johnston, a friend of Terry's requested that the regiment join him in Tennessee. When the men arrived in Nashville one of the recruits, J.K.P. Blackburn, described the festive mood: "The news of our coming and stories of the marvelous acts of horsemanship of the cowboys had preceded us; and we proved to be a great attraction for the people of Nashville and surrounding country—so much so that crowds gathered in the mornings and greater crowds in the evenings every day while we were getting in our horses in that city."

The more skilled and daring Texans entertained the citizens. Blackburn recalled: "Every wild, unbroken, vicious horse in that section was brought in to be ridden. When one came in there was generally a rush made by the soldiers to get first chance at him. When he had been bridled and saddled one would mount him, pull off the bridle, turn him loose, put spurs to him, and bid him do his worst. Before he was half through with the performance another soldier would spring upon him as a hind-rider and after a time, depending upon the strength of the animal, he would come to a stand-still, completely exhausted and his riders were ready for the next act."

Those Rangers who lacked this taste for adventure, however, took a more prudent approach to the wild animals.

Henry Graber, who watched the cowboys with much admiration, related that when his turn came to choose a horse he selected one from a line of around a thousand tied to a picket rope. Unfortunately, he recalled, "we had no time to take out a horse and try his gaits, and it proved largely guesswork in the selection of the horses." A "long swinging walk and fox trot" were the best gaits for a cavalry mount, Graber believed, but he had the bad luck to choose a pacer, an animal whose stride made every mile torture for the uncomfortable rider.

Many of the Texans proved superb horsemen who loved to perform. Leonidus B. Giles remembered that while his regiment camped at the fairgrounds in Nashville, "Ladies in great numbers visited us, and for their entertainment our most expert horsemen gave the first really-truly 'wild-west' entertainment ever seen east of the Mississippi." One trooper described a typical event: "To start this performance it would be announced from the stand…that a number of silver dollars would be strewn along on the race track for anyone that would run at full speed and pick them up. This proposition would create much rivalry and interest among those who had gotten their mounts" and were short of cash. Much to the delight of the crowds, the riders generally picked up the money on the first dash. "This extraordinary feat," wrote Henry Graber, "in connection with their general appearance; being armed with shotguns, six-shooters and Bowie knives, seemed to sustain their idea of the Texas Rangers that fought at the Alamo, Goliad and San Jacinto and served under Jack Hayes, Ben McCollough [sic] and other Indian and Mexican fighters." Another popular stunt of the Texans was to form in squads and ride "at a maddening gallop down the streets," while "jumping off & on their mounts and picking up pieces of cloth and sticks off the ground." In 1863 Colonel Fremantle watched a display of Texas prowess: "I saw them lasso cattle, and catch them by the tail at full gallop, and throw them by slewing them around.

This is called tailing. They pick small objects off the ground when at full tilt, and, in their peculiar fashion, are beautiful riders; but they confessed to me they could not ride in an English saddle, and Colonel [James] Duff told me that they could not jump a fence at all. They were all extremely anxious to hear what I thought of the performance, and their thorough good opinion of themselves was most amusing."

This peerless horsemanship meant that early in the war Texans enjoyed great success intimidating Federal troops. In the 8th Texas' first encounter with the enemy in December 1861 the commander of the Indiana Infantry recalled, "with lightning speed, under infernal yelling, great numbers of Texas rangers rushed upon our whole force. They advanced to fifteen or twenty yards of our lines, some of them even between them, and opened fire with rifles and revolvers." A letter found on a dead Federal soldier read: "The 'Texas Rangers' are as quick as lightning. They ride like Arabs, shoot like archers at a mark, and fight like devils. They rode upon our bayonets as if they were charging a commissary department, [and they] are wholly without fear themselves, and no respecters of a wish to surrender."

Despite their reputation, and although willing to charge when ordered, Texans preferred to do so only when they saw a chance of success, and even then they insisted that the person ordering the action be willing to risk his own life along with theirs. Sergeant Robert Hodges of the 8th Texas Cavalry wrote of his commanding officer: "I think that Col. Terry is pursuing a very unwise course...in fact I think he has acted the saphead ever since he left home." But after Terry died leading a brave but foolish charge, Hodges remembered him as "our gallant and beloved Col. Terry."

While the frontal assault remained popular, as weaponry improved the mounted charge with sabers raised almost disappeared. It did not take Texans long to realize that the dangers involved overshadowed the glamour of the saber charge. Moreover, because of the shortage of weapons, a "saber" could be anything from a hunting knife to a Bowie knife; only a few men owned regulation sabers. A member of the 3rd Texas Cavalry wrote: "Some of these knives were three feet long, and heavy enough to cleave the skull of a mailed knight through helmet and all." Another eager recruit in the 15th Texas Cavalry recalled that the knives were made out of "old scythe blades, plowshares, cross cut saws, or anything else that could be had. The blade was from two to three feet in length, and ground as sharp as could be." The men practiced with the weapons by racing through the brush, slicing the tops off of small pine trees, "so that we could lift [off] the heads of the Yankees artistically as soon as we could catch up with them."

While most of these homemade sabers soon disappeared, the skill the Texans developed while practicing mounted assaults had the desired effect. One of the many accounts published in Texas newspapers described a typical charge on a group of Yankees near Little Rock. Gil McKay of the 17th Texas Cavalry wrote, "our men commenced yelling, and for five minutes there was one of the most unearthly screams that I ever hear—it was fearful." It had the right effect for "when the enemy first saw us," recalled McKay, "they thought we were 'Arkansawyers'...[but] their commander told them that 'they were the d—m Texans,' to look out for themselves." The "Feds skedaddled"—a term McKay explained meant "to cut dirt."

Many Texans quickly discarded the saber in favor of the pistols and shotguns they brought from home. Shotguns were common in Texas, and since the men had to furnish their own arms it was the weapon of choice for many. Some even had double-barreled weapons which, in the hands of fast-moving cavalry units, inflicted greater damage than a rifle. In fact, late in the war some Texas cavalrymen preferred their shotguns even when they had the opportunity to exchange them for something better. A twelve-gauge shotgun with a thirty-two-inch barrel loaded with buckshot will bury pellets into a tree at one hundred yards. Although at that distance the pellets will spread about seven feet, they could do significant damage to a man. Moreover, the chances of hitting something was greatly increased, especially if the man's mount proved an excitable or jumpy horse. At short range the shotgun was particularly lethal.

As the war progressed, some cavalrymen exchanged their shotguns for Federal carbines. By 1864 a few of the Texans with the Army of Tennessee had captured popular breech-loading Spencers. The short-barreled .52-caliber Spencer repeating carbine delivered seven shots in less than thirty seconds. Its advanced design took a magazine-fed primed-rimfire cartridge. This newly invented moisture-proof metal cartridge replaced the combustible paper or linen one, and eliminated the need for percussion caps. Confederates often lacked the equipment to make these cartridges, however, and when they ran out of captured ammunition were forced to return to the shotgun.

Despite this drawback, for obvious reasons, captured weapons were popular. Another cavalry arm was the .52-caliber Sharps carbine. Southern factories manufactured a copy of the Union weapon, and it became the most common of the Confederate breechloaders. In the Trans-Mississippi some Texas units eventually received the Confederate Sharps, a simple paper-cartridge breechloader that did not require the special rimfire cartridge. Unfortunately, one Southern general complained that the Richmond Sharps was "so defective as to be demoralizing to our men," probably an understatement since in one test seven of nine barrels burst. Even Union cavalry commander Judson Kilpatrick complained in January 1865 that "the majority of my Sharps carbines, are utterly worthless." He asked James H. Wilson, Chief of Cavalry, to send him 300 Spencer carbines, "with as little delay as possible."

The Texans had originally planned to use another

questionable weapon, the lance, on a large scale. In November 1861 the *Texas State Gazette* announced the formation of a regiment of mounted lancers. The advertisement read, "This will be the only Regiment of Lancers in the service, and Lancers are the most formidable cavalry in the world.... The lance simply takes the place of the sword in a charge, and is much the more terrible weapon."

The use of lances was not as novel as many Texans imagined. Confederate General Joseph E. Johnston favored increasing Southern cavalry and alleviating the shortage of arms by "equipping a large body of lancers." Even Federal General Henry W. Halleck emphasized that in a charge the lance or saber often proved superior to a pistol or carbine. "In a regular charge the lance offers great advantages," Halleck wrote. Moreover, he claimed that "in the mêlée the saber is the best weapon; hence some miliary writers have proposed arming the front rank with lances, and the second with sabers." Major General Joseph Wheeler's popular cavalry manual described how a man would defend himself against the lance. Noting that it was the common weapon of Indians, Wheeler maintained that defense "depends much upon horsemanship, [and] the judgment of the rider." Successful maneuvers, he claimed, were similar to those used for the bow and arrow, thus Texans should be extremely proficient in this type of warfare.

For Texans anxious to join the cavalry in the spring of 1862 this seemed logical enough. True, Indians used lances, and Mexicans had used lances in the Mexican War. It is fortunate, however, that the lances never arrived. Lances against Federals, particularly those armed with modern weapons, would have been suicidal.

Three regiments of Texas lancers raised by George Washington Carter, a former Methodist preacher, proved to be notoriously undisciplined. Charged with taking his men to Arkansas, Colonel Carter simply did not have time, or failed to take time, to make soldiers out of these rowdy Texans. Even if he had disciplined them, Carter knew virtually nothing about being a soldier and that became readily apparent in his men. Trouble began as soon as the brigade left Houston and headed for Arkansas. At Shreveport, Louisiana, charges were brought against one of the colonels for "continual drunkenness and other improprieties, and [for fighting] in a grog shop...with one of his own men." Louisiana Governor Thomas O. Moore complained to the secretary of war that these Texans were terrorizing his state. He claimed they had "seized private property, entered houses of private citizens, brutally practiced extortion and outrage, and with bullying and threatening language and manner spread terror among the people." The manner in which they carried out their supposed mission, to obtain supplies for the army in Arkansas, had angered many Louisiana citizens. To prevent similar occurrences, Moore ordered out the state militia and warned the secretary of war: "You can refuse to dismiss [the men involved], but my marksmen may save you the trouble [of arresting them] if they come again. There is a point to which patient endurance can extend no further."

Unfortunately, lack of discipline characterized many Texas troops, partly because of the democratic makeup of the units. Most Texas cavalrymen preferred to remain in the ranks and never applied for promotion. One Texan recalled that when his company was organized "the noncommissioned officers were distributed among the different sections from which the company was made up; nobody caring for an office of any kind, as a private was generally the equal of any officer in command."

Most commanders remained tolerant of minor infractions, partly because they had little choice. When Colonel Carter declared he would lash anyone caught stealing, the rebellious troops threatened to mutiny. A captain complained: "The idea that a soldier, a volunteer soldier, would be publicly whipped by stripes on the bare back—was not to be considered—no matter how many hogs and chickens, ducks and turkey[s] he stole." Carter gave in, and in fact he seldom punished his men for infractions of the rules. The troops liked him, and he certainly tried to create the image Texans expected. He dressed like a West Texas cowboy, wearing a coonskin cap,

John Austin Wharton: born Tennessee 1828; family ties in Texas prompted his parents to move there the next year; attended South Carolina College (University of South Carolina); returned to Texas to practice law; member of the Texas Secession Convention; with the outbreak of Civil War, he went to Virginia to offer his services to the Confederacy; returned to Texas where he was commissioned captain in the 8th Texas Cavalry (Terry's Texas Rangers); elevated to colonel after Frank Terry's death; led the regiment with distinction and was wounded at Shiloh; recovered in

time to command his regiment in the Kentucky Campaign; brigadier general 1862; he headed a brigade at Murfreesboro and Chickamauga; promoted to major general in 1863; disagreements with another cavalry commander, Major General Joseph Wheeler, resulted in friction in the Army of Tennessee, and Wharton applied for a transfer to the Trans-Mississippi; while on leave from General Joseph E. Johnston's army, he assumed command of Major General Richard Taylor's cavalry after the death of Brigadier General Tom Green at Blair's Landing in April 1864; Taylor said that Wharton would "lead the gallant sons of Texas to victory." His troopers relentlessly harassed the retreating Federals for the remainder of the Red River Campaign; spent the balance of the war in the Trans-Mississippi. In 1865, following an altercation at Major General John B. Magruder's Houston headquarters, an unarmed Wharton was shot to death by fellow Texan, Colonel George W. Baylor. When Wharton had joined the Confederate army in Louisiana, General Taylor had remarked that he arrived "with crown adorned with the laurels of many a hard-fought field," and he would take his "place at once in the front ranks of Texas leaders."

wrapping himself in a striped tiger blanket, and sporting fancy top boots.

Moreover, Texans preferred non-professional soldiers like themselves, and did not hesitate to question the wisdom of officers with genuine military training. Texans frequently judged situations from a practical point of view, and firmly believed they had a right to disregard orders they deemed unwise. Lieutenant William Walton of the 21st Texas related an incident during the Red River Campaign aptly expressing the Texans' reluctance to follow orders they considered foolhardy. He recalled that during a skirmish his detachment ran out of ammunition and he instructed his men to take cover in a drainage ditch to wait for reinforcements. When General William Steele rode up he saw a line over a mile long standing idle and angrily asked the lieutenant why he had halted his pursuit. Walton explained his situation to the West Pointer, but Steele ordered the Texans, in a still "rougher & harsher voice," to attack. Walton, who knew he had to obey or face arrest, recalled: "We rode out of the ditch & charged, without a loaded gun in the ranks." It was a stroke of luck that the Federals had already begun to retreat and thus no one was hurt, but Walton complained, "being no educated soldier, I'll take to the ditch.... We were not cowards—we did not run—stood our ground—but were for the time invisible to the enemy. Irregular! may be so—but I had rather be a little irregular than to be shot to pieces being regular."

This incident occurred in Louisiana, but lack of discipline extended beyond the limits of the Trans-Mississippi. While serving with the Confederate army in Tennessee, John Austin Wharton, who rose to major general of cavalry, discovered just how far he could push his fellow Texans before the men resisted. When he ordered an enlisted man to drive a wagon, the trooper balked, although his selection had come after a democratic drawing of lots. The soldier's brusque refusal created a temporary crisis, but Wharton resolved the matter without a general revolt in the command by hiring a volunteer to drive the mules at fifty dollars per month.

The willful, often headstrong, independence exhibited by many Southern cavalrymen exasperated Confederate generals. Braxton Bragg, who headed the Army of Tennessee, frequently reminded his cavalry commander Major General Joseph Wheeler that he would not allow the pillaging and straggling common among the horsemen. When warnings failed to reform the recalcitrant troopers, Bragg lost patience with this unruly branch of his army, and vowed that those caught would be dismounted and assigned to the infantry. He understood that walking was unacceptable to most horsemen, and this punishment would represent the harshest possible penalty.

No trooper wanted to exchange his horse for a pair of marching boots. A man mounted on a horse, armed with a shotgun or carbine, knew he had a certain amount of independence that the foot soldier lacked. This sense of freedom often meant that cavalrymen lived on the edge of military propriety, and Texans, in particular, became notorious for ignoring or altering orders to meet the situations they encountered. Nonetheless, what the Texans lacked in military refinement they made up in pure nerve. Their success in battle encouraged army commanders to overlook many infractions, and allowed them a latitude not generally granted the average soldier.

4

"TEXIANS" IN THE
RED RIVER CAMPAIGN

On numerous occasions during the Civil War Texas cavalrymen proved their willingness to fight, but never with more courage and suffering than during the Red River Campaign of 1864. As the year began, Abraham Lincoln's government began to devise strategy for a major offensive west of the Mississippi River, a plan to invade Arkansas and Louisiana in an attempt to gain control of the cotton fields of East Texas. Victories in this part of the Confederacy could eliminate Arkansas and Louisiana from any further participation in the war, and a Federal presence in the region might arouse Texas Unionism. Moreover, an invasion could possibly strangle the profitable Confederate trade with Mexico that flourished along the Rio Grande border. Perhaps more important, Lincoln needed a meaningful victory as the

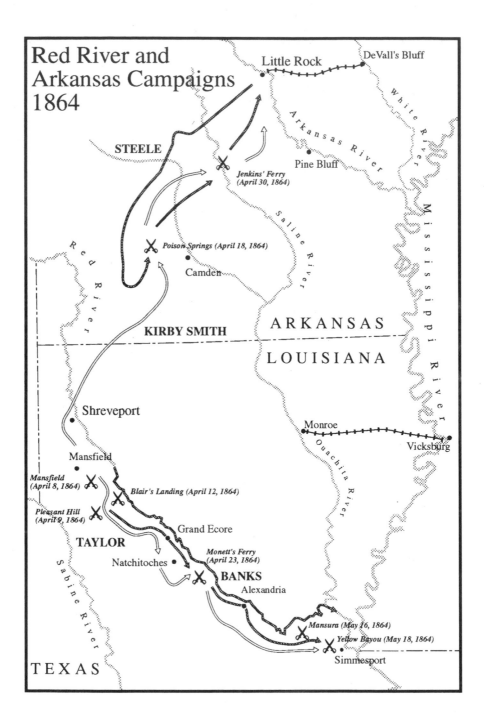

Red River and Arkansas Campaigns 1864

presidential election in November was only months away.

In March the newly appointed Union General-in-Chief Ulysses S. Grant planned a coordinated assault upon the major Confederate armies. In Virginia General George G. Meade's Army of the Potomac would move against General Robert E. Lee's Army of Northern Virginia, while in Georgia General

Andrew Jackson Smith: born Pennsylvania 1815; graduated U. S. Military Academy in 1838, thirty-sixth in his class of forty-five; commissioned 2d lieutenant and posted to 1st Dragoons; saw service on the western frontier and in

the Mexican War; 1st lieutenant 1845; captain 1847; major 1861; colonel and chief of cavalry to Major General Henry Halleck during his advance on Corinth, Mississippi, 1862; brigadier general U.S. Volunteers 1862; commanded a division in Major General William T. Sherman's attack on Chickasaw Bluffs and throughout the Vicksburg Campaign of 1863; detached to support Major General Nathaniel P. Banks' Red River Expedition in the Spring of 1864; defeated Confederates at Pleasant Hill, Louisiana, but was angered by the campaign's overall failure and Banks' ineffectiveness; major general U.S. Volunteers, May 1864; still detached, he won an independent action at Tupelo, Mississippi, before moving into Missouri and finally Tennessee; joined Major General George Thomas' command in the rout of General John B. Hood's force at Nashville in December 1864; led the Sixteenth Corps in the operations against Mobile 1865; breveted brigadier general U.S. Army for Pleasant Hill and major general for Nashville; continuing in the service after the war, he became colonel of the 7th U.S. Cavalry; resigned his commission 1869; in civil service in St. Louis; placed on the retired list in 1889 by the Army with the rank of colonel of cavalry; died at St. Louis in 1897. Although not as recognized as many of his contemporaries, General Smith was nonetheless one of the most capable officers to serve the Union. He proved as equally effective in a subordinate role or in independent action. His soldiers were among the hardest marchers and toughest fighters on either side during the war.

William T. Sherman's forces would move against General Joseph E. Johnston's Army of Tennessee. Sherman planned to head for Atlanta where, if all went well, he would join Federal forces pushing in from Mobile, Alabama. But this plan never completely materialized. By the time Grant took over, the outgoing supreme commander Henry W. Halleck had already put in motion a scheme of his own. He scrapped the Mobile invasion in favor of an expedition into the Trans-Mississippi,

David Dixon Porter: born Pennsylvania 1813; son of Commodore David Porter, he accompanied his father's pirate suppression expeditions in the Gulf of Mexico; having spent much of his early life at sea, he received little formal education; joined the Mexican Navy as a midshipman in 1827, joined U.S. Navy as

midshipman in 1829; lieutenant 1841; saw considerable service during the Mexican War; served various merchant enterprises but returned to active duty in 1855; with the outbreak of Civil War, served in blockade squadrons; promoted to commander in 1861 after twenty years as a lieutenant; capably led the mortar flotilla in the capture of New Orleans; given command of the Mississippi River Squadron in October 1862; for his excellent service during the Vicksburg Campaign he was elevated to rear admiral, bypassing the ranks of captain and commodore; took a large fleet up the Red River to support Major General Nathaniel P. Banks' ill-fated campaign; the fleet was harassed by Confederate land forces and slowed by low water levels during its difficult retreat; sent East, he directed the North Atlantic Squadron for the balance of the war, participating in the capture of Fort Fisher, North Carolina; superintendent of the United States Naval Academy, 1865-1869; vice admiral 1866; admiral 1870; author of numerous books including *Incidents of the Civil War* (1886) and *History of the Navy During the War of the Rebellion* (1890); he died 1891. The failure of the Red River Expedition notwithstanding, Admiral Porter played a significant role in the Federal success in the West. He was the cousin of Major General Fitz-John Porter.

where cotton might be secured for the mills of New England. General Nathaniel P. Banks, in charge of the Department of the Gulf, had orders to move up the Red River together with a powerful naval force, while General Frederick Steele marched south from Little Rock, both armies heading for Shreveport.

Richard Taylor: born Kentucky 1826; son of President and Mexican War hero Zachary Taylor and brother-in-law of Confederate President Jefferson Davis; studied at Yale; became a successful sugar planter in Louisiana; elected colonel 9th Louisiana Infantry at the outbreak of the Civil War and went with the regiment to Virginia, arriving too late for First Manassas; promoted to brigadier general 1861; commanded the Louisiana Brigade in Major General Thomas J. "Stonewall" Jackson's Shenandoah Valley Campaign of 1862; present but not active during the Seven Days' Battles before Richmond; promoted to major general and assigned to command the District of Western Louisiana in 1862; unsuccessfully opposed Major General Nathaniel P. Banks' Bayou Teche Expedition in 1863, but turned back Banks' Red River Expedition the following spring; after a heated exchange in which he criticized his commander, General E. Kirby Smith, for not following up this success, he asked to be relieved; he was, however, promoted to lieutenant general and assigned to command the Department of Alabama, Mississippi, and East Louisiana; following the disaster at Nashville, he temporarily succeeded General John B. Hood in command of the Army of Tennessee, most of  which he forwarded to the Carolinas to oppose Major General William T. Sherman's advance; after the fall of Mobile he surrendered the last remaining Confederate force east of the Mississippi to Major General E.R.S. Canby on May 4, 1865; following the war he was active in Democratic politics and vigorously opposed Reconstruction policies; died at New York in 1879. That year he published *Destruction and Reconstruction*, one of the finest participant memoirs to be produced. Without any formal military training, General Taylor proved to be a most able commander. The Confederate repulse of the Red River Expedition, though largely overlooked, was a major achievement.

Grant's promotion came too late for him to influence this decision, and he later wrote that he had "opposed the movement strenuously, but acquiesced because it was the order of my superior at the time."

General Grant had hoped the joint army-navy expedition up the Red River would be over before his own spring offensive began. To expedite matters, Sherman donated some 10,000 infantry and several artillery units for the movement, while General Alfred W. Ellet contributed about 1,000 men of his Marine Brigade (an army unit despite the name) all under the command of hardened veteran General Andrew J. Smith. To meet the deadline for the Georgia campaign, Sherman's, troops were to be returned to the Army of the Tennessee 30 days after their arrival on the Red River. Rear Admiral David D. Porter brought thirteen ironclads, four tinclads, and five other armed vessels with him for service on the Red River. With the army transport and quartermaster boats, there were some 60 Federal ships with over 200 guns. Both Smith and Porter were to join almost 20,000 soldiers from the Department of the Gulf at Alexandria, Louisiana, and then head for Shreveport where they would unite with Steele's force of over 11,000 Arkansas troops.

Nathaniel Banks' Federal army never reached Shreveport. To meet the Union advance, Confederate General Richard Taylor quickly amassed all available troops. His motley force defeated Banks at the Battle of Sabine Crossroads near Mansfield on April 8, 1864, and vigorously engaged the Federal army at Pleasant Hill the following day. Historian Ludwell Johnson concluded: "Tactically, the battle of Pleasant Hill was distinctly a Northern victory, although the retreat to Grand Ecore turned it into a strategic defeat." Banks' decision to withdraw proved fortunate for the Confederates, as General Edmund Kirby Smith, commander of the Trans-Mississippi Department, pulled back most of Taylor's infantry, sending it north to check Frederick Steele's drive south from Little Rock.

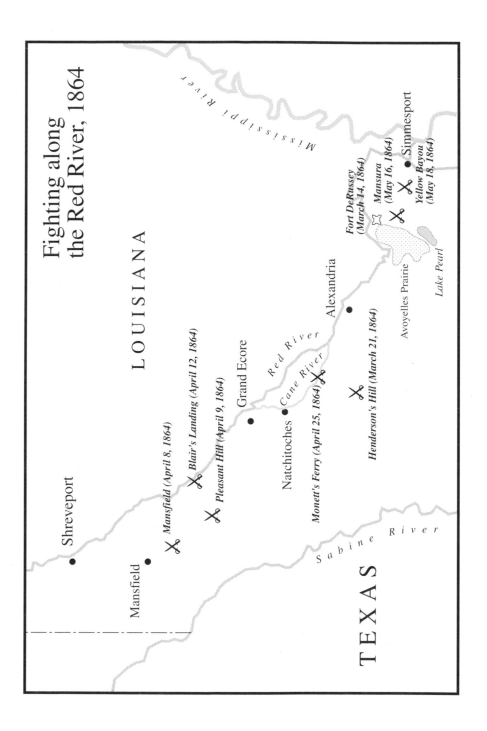

Fighting along
the Red River, 1864

William Henry Parsons: born New Jersey 1826; of Puritan stock, but "by training and preference a fervent, even fanatical, Southerner"; spent his childhood in Montgomery, Alabama, where his father ran a grocery store and William "thrived in an environment that respected a skilled horseman or marksman far more than a scholar"; by the time he reached manhood "his political convictions reflected attitudes prevalent throughout the South"; studied at Emory College in Georgia, but quit school in 1844 and joined the 2d U.S. Dragoons commanded by Zachary Taylor; settled in Texas following the Mexican War; bought a newspaper in Tyler and at age twenty-six became an editor; known as a talented writer whose editorials reflected courage and conviction; moved to the Brazos River region in central Texas; favored reopening the slave trade and building a transcontinental railroad through Texas; in 1860 founded a pro-Southern newspaper in Waco and warned Texans to arm themselves for conflict if Abraham Lincoln won the presidency; after Texas seceded, Parsons raised the 4th Texas Dragoons (later designated the 12th Texas

Cavalry), which elected him colonel; moved with his regiment to Arkansas where it turned back a Federal advance toward Little Rock and earned "a reputation for daring fighting that endured throughout the war"; in 1862 became commander of Parsons' Cavalry Brigade, prominent during various actions in Arkansas and Louisiana, especially the Red River Campaign of 1864; the Confederate Congress never promoted Parsons to brigadier general, yet he acted in that capacity for much of the conflict. After the war, Parsons went to South America, but soon returned to Texas and served in the state senate from 1869 to 1871; he moved to New York in 1871 after President Ulysses S. Grant appointed him U.S. Centennial Commissioner; thereafter he held various government jobs. Colonel Parsons, called "Wild Bill" by his troopers, liked to recall "his military service and noted that he had the distinction of repelling two invasions of Texas, first on the Rio Grande under Zachary Taylor and later on the Red River under Zachary's son Richard. He believed that his skill in sword exercise and field maneuvers learned during the war with Mexico gave him the advantage over other Confederate field commanders drawn straight from civilian life." He died in Chicago in 1907.

This left mainly cavalry, under the command of the capable General Thomas Green, to keep an eye on Porter's vessels.

Parsons' Texas Cavalry Brigade, en route from Texas, unfortunately failed to arrive in time to participate at either Sabine Crossroads or Pleasant Hill. The Texans were veterans

Nathaniel Macon Burford: born Tennessee 1824; began teaching in a country school at age seventeen, and by 1845 had graduated from Irving College and Lebanon Law School; gave up his small law practice to volunteer for the Mexican War, but by the time his company assembled in Knoxville, the state had filled its required quota; determined to fight—his brother was with General Winfield Scott's army—Burford left home hoping to enlist in Texas; he worked his way to Shreveport, Louisiana, as a deck hand, and walked from there to Jefferson, Texas; with only three dollars in his pocket, he took a job as deputy clerk of the district court instead of joining the army; in 1848, Burford moved to Dallas and established a law practice where he soon formed a partnership with another Tennessean, John H. Reagan; in the 1850s, Burford was elected Dallas district attorney, then district judge, and helped draft the Dallas city charter; he was an advocate of states' rights and supported the legality of slavery; in 1861, he enlisted as a private in the 1st Texas Artillery under the command of John J. Good, a fellow judge and friend, who wrote that Burford "does his part like a man and is now one of the finest specimens of a cornfield hand you ever saw."

Colonel Good regarded Burford as a model soldier and sought to have him promoted: "He never fails to do any duty required of him day or night." Discharged from the 1st Texas Artillery and authorized to raise a regiment, Burford recruited the 19th Texas Cavalry, and was elected colonel; criticized for neglecting his men and drinking, Burford failed to prepare his regiment for combat; although he fought in the Red River Campaign, he resigned at its conclusion; speaker of the Texas House of Representatives after the war, later a county and district judge, and United States commissioner; he died in Dallas in 1898. Slightly built with dark brown hair and soft gray eyes, he was "an affable, genial man, generous to his own detriment, ...and though not a poet, had much of poetry in his nature."

and Taylor could have used their added numbers. The men of the brigade, under the command of Colonel William Henry Parsons, had earned a reputation as formidable fighters over the past two years.

Parsons' Brigade consisted of Parsons' own 12th Texas Cavalry, Nathaniel M. Burford's 19th Texas Cavalry, George W. Carter's 21st Texas Cavalry, Charles Morgan's Cavalry Battalion, and Joseph H. Pratt's Texas Battery. The 12th Regiment remained the brigade's backbone; the 19th and 21st regiments had not officially organized until the spring of 1862, and were never as proficient soldiers as the men in the 12th Texas. Colonel Burford, who had served early in the war with Ben McCulloch, was a former county judge from Dallas. Moreover, he had the advantage of political connections in the Confederate capital, for the Confederate postmaster general, John H. Reagan, had once been his law partner. Colonel Carter —the same who had been unable to discipline his troops on the way to Arkansas in 1862—hailed from Virginia, where he had strong connections in Richmond. Neither Carter nor Burford had the ability to lead troops; whereas Burford eventually realized this and resigned, Carter never did. Carter also claimed to outrank Parsons, and thus believed he should command the brigade. This dispute caused numerous problems during the ensuing campaign.

In Arkansas, Parsons' duties had involved reconnaissance and the harassment of Union foraging trains and scouting parties. The 12th Texas defended Little Rock when General Samuel R. Curtis' Union Army of the Southwest marched through the state in 1862. In the spring of 1863, part of the brigade participated in General John S. Marmaduke's unsuccessful raid into Missouri. Later that summer the Texans rode to Louisiana, where they attacked Federal garrisons and destroyed plantations operated by the United States government along the Mississippi River in an unsuccessful effort to aid the defenders at Vicksburg.

These Texans, bold and aggressive, preferred the offensive. In almost every skirmish from Missouri to Louisiana, they struck first, often utilizing the element of surprise to ensure victory. As cavalry, they loved a glorious charge with sabers drawn, and they gained a reputation along the Mississippi River for their fearless, and often ferocious, style of fighting. One Texas officer noted: "Our men are cautious, but when they make a fight, they fight like devils. The Yankees call them 'Hell Yelpers,' from the fact that they always raise the war whoop when they fight." In 1862 a member of the brigade noted that

Harper's New Monthly Magazine published this sketch of the Confederate attack on Porter's fleet at Blair's Landing.

the Federals "have a wholesome dread of the Texans—they dont like our mode of fighting. I believe the Texans mode of fighting is to hurt somebody no matter how that is." Likewise, a Union private wrote, "fighting the Texans is like walking into a den of wildcats."

Despite their pugnacious qualities, the Texas cavalrymen often appeared less disciplined than wildcats. General Taylor, under whom they now fought, had once observed: "Officers and men addressed each other as Tom, Dick, or Harry, and had no more conception of military graduations than of the celestial hierarchy of the poets." Yet he acknowledged, "the men were hardy and many of the officers brave and zealous" although "the value of these qualities was lessened by lack of discipline."

But Taylor had little time to ponder the horsemen's inadequate military training. Admiral Porter, unaware of Banks' about-face and hasty retreat, continued to move his fleet upriver. About one mile above Loggy Bayou (located a little over halfway between Natchitoches and Shreveport), Porter found the river blocked. Taylor, attempting to delay the passage of the Federal fleet, had ordered a ship sunk in the channel. "It was," observed Porter, "the smartest thing I ever knew the rebels to do.... They had left an invitation to attend a ball in Shreveport which," he sadly recalled, "we were never able to accept." While trying to decide what he should do, the admiral sent men to reconnoiter the countryside. After soldiers reported sighting Southern cavalry, Porter concluded: "Banks has been defeated, or we wouldn't see those men here." Sure enough, on April 10, Lieutenant Frank L. Church, commanding the marine guard aboard Porter's flagship, wrote in his diary that the admiral had received "dispatches of very unfavorable character from General Banks."

As Porter prepared to withdraw his fleet, Taylor laid plans to destroy it. The narrow river channel made reversing directions difficult, forcing Porter to back the larger vessels downstream several miles to turn around. The admiral realized that the ships made easy marks for the Confederates, and every minute he lingered on the unfriendly waters increased his chances of destruction. Even after Porter had his vessels heading south, the flight toward Grand Ecore was plagued with mishaps as shallow water and frequent bends in the river caused several vessels to run aground. Taylor's first attempt to intercept the fleet with a mounted column under Arthur P. Bagby failed, but General Tom Green headed the second column himself. Green led part of Parsons' Brigade, two untested Texas cavalry regiments (the 23rd and 36th), and two small howitzers from West's Louisiana Battery toward the Red River. Riding out of Pleasant Hill, the mounted column included more than a thousand Texans. The cavalrymen were ready to take on the U.S. Navy.

5

LONE STAR HORSEMEN AND THE U.S. NAVY

The fleet's retreat down the Red River rapidly became an agonizing ordeal for the men aboard the vessels as the swift current and low water level made navigation treacherous. Tree stumps and sandbars rose from the murky water, ready to shatter the wooden-bottomed boats. On the morning of April 12, two of the vessels collided, forcing a delay for repairs. By afternoon most of the vessels had passed Blair's Landing, about forty-five miles above Grand Ecore, but five transports and two gunboats had to stop. One ship tied up at the landing to fix its wheel; another, carrying 400 horses, grounded in midstream, and two transports went to its assistance. Upstream, the powerful monitor *Osage* also ran aground. As the gunboat *Lexington* lingered near the landing waiting for Commodore Thomas O. Selfridge to float the *Osage*,

Confederate sharpshooters appeared along the river's banks. Lieutenant Church noted in his diary that one of the vessels had been fired upon by "200 or 300 guerrillas with muskets."

The stop for repairs made everyone edgy. Continual harassment from Southern marksmen only served to remind the Federals that it was simply a matter of time before the Confederates mounted a serious attack. When Green's force arrived at Blair's Landing late in the afternoon of April 12, a pilot on a transport lashed to the *Osage* sent a warning to the soldiers on board. Commodore Selfridge later wrote: "I ascended to the pilot-house and from their being dressed in Federal overcoats thought they were our troops; but soon their movements—dismounting and picketing their horses—

Thomas Oliver Selfridge: born Massachusetts 1836; graduated U.S. Naval Academy first in his class of 1854; passed midshipman 1856; master 1858; lieutenant 1860; present at the destruction of the Norfolk Navy Yard in 1861; commanded the forward battery on the U.S. frigate *Cumberland* in its battle with the *Merrimack* (*Virginia*) in March 1862; lieutenant commander 1862; joined the Mississippi River Squadron for the Vicksburg Campaign; during the Red River Expedition of 1864 he was instrumental in the dam building operations that allowed the Federal fleet to continue; with Admiral David Dixon Porter he joined the North Atlantic Squadron; conspicuously involved in the capture of Fort Fisher, North Carolina, in 1865; continuing in the U.S. Navy following the war, he was promoted to commander in 1869; participated in numerous surveys in Central and South America, including that of the Darien Isthmus (Panama) for which he received the Legion of Honor of France;

captain 1881; commodore 1894; rear admiral 1896; retired 1898. Admiral Selfridge died in 1924; his memoirs were published the same year. Selfridge had a knack for being where the action was; he was involved in an amazing number of the Navy's most important events.

convinced me they were enemies." As the Confederates reached the river, Colonel Parsons, under the watchful eye of General Green, took command. Dismounting all but 400 of the troops, Parsons gave the order to charge, and the Texans "swept with a true rebel yell across the fence and through the field to the river bank in front of the enemy's vessels." Commodore Selfridge recalled: "Then commenced one of the most curious fights of the war, 2,500 infantry against a gunboat aground." But as the Confederates reached the river they saw the gunboat in motion, and assumed this meant a Federal retreat. David W. Fentress, assistant surgeon with Colonel Parsons, noted that the Texans "gave a hearty cheer" as they waved their arms in victory. But their mistake soon became apparent. Instead of withdrawing, the enemy opened the gun ports on their vessels and began bombarding the river. The bank, about forty feet high, gave way beneath the heavy blows as the shells enfiladed the Confederate line, and many Texans tumbled down to the water.

Despite heavy firing, Parsons' troops sustained few casualties. One observer described "shells bursting around, solid shot ploughing the ground, grape, canister and minnie balls whistling through the ranks." But Parsons' veterans, accustomed to fighting gunboats along the Mississippi and Arkansas rivers, proved hard to hit. The men lay on their backs while loading their weapons, affording a target only when they rose to charge. At the height of the action Parsons received an order to retreat, an order that he believed came from General Green. But as the men began to pull back, a brother of Green exclaimed: "Great God, Colonel! What does this mean?" Parsons replied, "I am ordered by General Green to withdraw my men." Green's brother responded, "Sir, this cannot be, for my brother lies yonder dead." Parsons immediately put spurs to his horse, and persuaded his men to head back for the river.

The Confederates had indeed lost their commander. Commodore Selfridge claimed that he had noticed an officer on a white horse about two hundred yards below the main line and, after aiming one of the guns at him, "saw him no longer. I learned after that the officer killed was their General Green." As soon as Colonel Parsons learned of Green's death, he believed the "entire responsibility of any further movement" fell upon his shoulders. Brigadier General James Major, seated on his horse at the left of the line, knew that Green had delegated field command to Parsons and did not intervene.

The fighting lasted until darkness compelled the Confederates to withdraw. General Major, as the ranking officer on the field, finally ordered Parsons to retreat. But the safety of the timber was over a mile from the river, and even in the darkness, the Texans, on foot, drew fire from the gunboats and from Federal infantry that had landed on the opposite bank. Nevertheless, Colonel Parsons' men retired in perfect order.

Since some of their vessels had sustained serious damage, the Federals declined to renew the action. During the battle the pilot of the transport *Black Hawk* discovered he could not escape from the iron pilot-house because of the intensity of the firing. When the contest ended, no fewer than sixty bullet marks dented the shield behind which he had hidden. Commodore Selfridge recalled: "One regiment would come up, deliver its fire then fall back under cover, and another advance." In his official report Selfridge added: "The rebels fought with unusual pertinacity for over an hour, delivering the heaviest and most concentrated fire of musketry that I have ever witnessed." Colonel Parsons claimed that even Admiral Porter admitted the Texans' "desperate courage baffled description."

After the Confederate withdrawal, Porter's vessels steamed south, docking at Grand Ecore a few days later. The Texans had not destroyed the squadron, but they had hurried Porter along in his retreat. A Union soldier who saw the vessels recorded in his diary: "The sides of some of the transports are half shot away, and their smoke-stacks look like huge pepper boxes."

Taylor had achieved a temporary success, but Green's death placed a burden on him. He needed to reorganize his troops quickly if he was to continue his pursuit down the river. Fortunately Major General John A. Wharton, recently transferred to the Trans-Mississippi from the Army of Tennessee, arrived at Shreveport soon after the skirmish at Blair's Landing, and at once took command of the cavalry. The thirty-five-year-old Wharton, whose Texas roots dated to the days of Mexican rule, had fought with the 8th Texas Cavalry (better known as Terry's Texas Rangers) in Kentucky in 1861. After Colonel Terry's death, Wharton eventually took command, leading the regiment at Shiloh. He later commanded a brigade at Stones River and Chickamauga, and received promotion to major general for valiant services.

In addition, Brigadier General William Steele arrived from Texas, where he had commanded the defenses at Galveston. Steele was a graduate of West Point whose military education had been furthered in the Mexican War, during which he had earned a brevet for bravery. As a regular army officer, he also had experience fighting Indians on the frontier. But unlike the Texan Wharton, the New York-born Steele had to work to gain and keep the respect of the skeptical soldiers from Texas. Nevertheless, Steele held the rank of brigadier general while Parsons remained a colonel; therefore, Steele assumed command over Parsons' Brigade.

Wharton and Steele arrived just as Taylor prepared to push Banks down the Red River, but the Federal general had already decided it was time to move toward Alexandria. Two important reasons influenced this decision. First, the river was rapidly falling, threatening the safety of Porter's vessels and making an advance virtually impossible. Second, and equally critical to Banks' program, was the need to return on schedule the men borrowed from Sherman. Banks, therefore, ordered A.J.

Smith's veteran western troops to cover the army's retreat. Back in March, Captain Elijah P. Petty of the 17th Texas Infantry Regiment had written to his wife: "If they advance with these forces we of necessity must retire until reinforced. If they retreat we will perhaps dog after them and try to bite their heels." Petty could not have known that the Confederates would make a stand at Mansfield, and that he would die at Pleasant Hill the next day. But his prediction was coming true; the Southern cavalry was now indeed biting at the heels of the enemy.

At Monett's Ferry, where Banks had to cross the Cane River, Taylor had a chance to encircle the Union army while it remained isolated from the protection of Porter's gunboats. Although the plan failed, Parsons' troops persistently attacked the tail of Banks' column, dogging the enemy's rear. In one

This flag, measuring 34 x 42 inches, belonged to the troopers in Parsons' Brigade. It may have been the one presented to the 12th Texas (originally the 4th Texas Dragoons) in late December 1861 when the regiment was in the vicinity of Houston.

Nathaniel P. Banks: born Massachusetts 1816; received little formal education; admitted to the bar in 1829; entered Massachusetts legislature, rising to speaker of the house; presided over the state's 1853 Constitutional Convention and was elected to the U.S. House of Representatives that same year; speaker of the House 1856; elected governor of Massachusetts in 1858, serving until 1861; at the outbreak of the Civil War, he offered his services to the Union and was appointed major general U.S. Volunteers by President Abraham Lincoln; headed the Department of Annapolis before assuming command of the Department of

the Shenandoah; prevented from reinforcing General G.B. McClellan on the Peninsula by the aggressive actions of General T.J. Jackson's Confederates in the Shenandoah Valley; defeated Jackson at Kernstown, Virginia, in March 1862, but fared poorly in subsequent actions; assigned to command the Second Corps in General John Pope's newly-formed Army of Virginia; defeated by Jackson at Cedar Mountain during the Second Bull Run Campaign in August 1862; after Pope's army was dismantled, Banks headed briefly the Military District of Washington before assuming command of the Department of the Gulf; conducted a costly operation against Port Hudson, which fell only after Vicksburg's capture left it untenable; directed the marginally successful Bayou Teche Expedition in the fall of 1863; following the failure of his Red River Expedition in 1864, Banks was relieved by General E.R.S. Canby; received thanks of Congress for Port Hudson; mustered out of volunteer service in 1865; returned to Congress where he served six more terms (not consecutively); declining health forced his retirement from Congress in 1890; he died in Massachusetts in 1894. General Banks was among the most active of the higher-ranking "political" generals. He was consistently placed in command positions that were beyond his abilities; his personal courage, devotion, and tenacity could not overcome his lack of military training.

charge, Private Henry Orr recalled, the Texans put the spurs to their horses and with the loud Texas yell, "bounded away as fast as our steeds could carry us." After driving the Federals from their position, the Texans held on for about an hour before being overpowered. Orr boasted: "Gen. Wharton said of our charge (though on a small scale), that he never saw it equalled on the other side of the River." Colonel Parsons agreed. It was, he believed, "one of the most brilliant and daring of the war."

Banks, nevertheless, successfully reached Alexandria. He was back at his starting point, and the Confederates could not have been more pleased. Private John P. Blessington of the 16th Texas Infantry could smugly contemplate an entry he had made in his diary on March 20, when he noted that Banks had plans of "crushing out or swallowing up our little army. It was the vain-glorious boast of the enemy at Alexandria, that before the end of April, all the 'rebel troops' in Louisiana and Arkansas would be driven into Texas." Now back at Alexandria, Banks discovered the fleet could not pass the rapids. Sections of the river had fallen to scarcely over three feet, and Porter required seven feet to carry his heavy gunboats over the falls. Porter's Mississippi squadron was stranded and, without a rise in the river, seemed doomed. Although Lieutenant Colonel Joseph Bailey offered a suggestion to dam the river, as was common in his Wisconsin logging country, Porter initially expressed no interest. In fact, he did not agree to the scheme until he began to suspect that Banks, whom he disliked and distrusted, might pull the army out of Alexandria. Porter feared waking up one morning and finding that Banks had deserted him. Several uneasy days followed before the fleet safely passed the falls—thanks to Bailey's ingenious dam.

Banks began his long march from Alexandria toward the Mississippi River on May 13. Over the next few days, Confederate horsemen constantly harassed the tired blue columns heading south. Two months had passed since Porter had first entered the mouth of the Red River; now the infantry labored to reach the site where the campaign had opened. But before the contest ended and the Confederates could claim a victory, the Southern horsemen would face one final test.

6

FIGHTING IN THE LOUISIANA BAYOUS

The Confederates, intent on driving the Federals out of Louisiana, followed Banks closely. As the cypress swamps and marshes increased, the Texans noted with distaste the endless trees clad in gray Spanish moss and morose, almost strangling vines. Pools of black water with mats of floating vegetation, slime, countless water moccasins, and an occasional alligator held no attraction for the Southern horsemen. Banks' desire to leave the Red River did not exceed the Texans' urge to flee the uninviting bayou country. But before Banks escaped there would be one more clash, a bloody battle on a muddy and sluggish little stream near the deserted village of Simmesport. Yellow Bayou, the closing engagement of the Red River campaign, was also the final combat for many of the Confederate horsemen.

Fighting began when the Federal commanders decided to quell the Confederate horsemen harassing their retreat. On May 17, when Texans assaulted the Union rear guard, Federal artillery replied with a heavy fire. Union General Joseph Mower, ordered by A.J. Smith to clear out the Rebels, took Colonel Sylvester Hill's Brigade, consisting of only the 33rd Missouri and the 35th Iowa, along with the brigades of Colonel William F. Lynch and Colonel William T. Shaw, and moved back to Yellow Bayou. These units were part of the veteran force on

Xavier Blanchard Debray: born France 1819; graduated from the French Military Academy before migrating to the United States in 1848; received his citizenship in 1855, at San Antonio, Texas, where he published a Spanish-language newspaper, and worked as a translator in the General Land Office at Austin; with the secession

of Texas, he joined the Tom Green Rifles as a 1st lieutenant, but was soon appointed aide-de-camp to Governor Francis R. Lubbock; eventually elected colonel 26th Texas Cavalry; during 1862, Debray commanded a sub-district in Texas that included Galveston, and was conspicuously engaged in the re-capture of that city in January 1863; his commander Major General John B. Magruder commended him for his "coolness and courage" as well as his leadership; in April 1864 Major General Richard Taylor wrote that "the soldierly qualities displayed by the Colonel, and the good conduct of his men, meet the acknowledgment of the Major-General commanding, who has every reason to form brilliant expectations of the future career of this fine corps." Debray and his regiment earned more praise at Mansfield and Pleasant Hill; although Debray was promoted to brigadier general by order of General E. Kirby Smith, in April 1864, President Jefferson Davis never made that appointment official; commanded a brigade of Texas cavalry until discharged, in March 1865; Debray eventually returned to his job at the General Land Office, and died at Austin 1895. A gifted cavalry officer, Debray spent the entire war in the obscurity of the Trans-Mississippi.

loan from Sherman. They had adequate artillery to hit the Southern cavalry, for accompanying Mower were the rifled guns of the 3rd Indiana Battery and four smoothbore guns of the 9th Indiana Battery.

Both sides knew this would be the last opportunity for the Confederates to engage the Federals before Banks' army

William Polk Hardeman: born Tennessee 1816; known as "Gotch" to his friends; moved to Texas in 1835 and settled in Matagorda County in 1838; took part in the Texas Revolution, and fought in several Indian campaigns in the 1830s and 1840s; represented Guadalupe County in the Texas Secession Convention, and was soon elected captain of a company in the 4th Texas Cavalry; Hardeman participated in Brigadier General Henry H. Sibley's invasion of New Mexico, leading at the Battle of Valverde "the last brilliant and successful charge, which decided the fortunes of that day." Promoted to lieutenant colonel and then to colonel of the 4th Texas, he was at the recapture of Galveston in 1863, and later accompanied Sibley to Louisiana; when the regiment became part of Brigadier General Thomas Green's command, Hardeman fought at Fort Bisland, Lafourche, Bayou Fordoche, and Bayou Bourbeau; in December 1863, the Texans headed home to protect the coast against a Union invasion, but in 1864 returned to Louisiana to participate in the Red River Campaign where Hardeman led his regiment at Mansfield and Pleasant Hill; after General Green's death at Blair's Landing, Hardeman  briefly commanded the cavalry; General E. Kirby Smith declared Hardeman a "pronounced superior" cavalryman—one of "the best brigade commanders in Trans-Mississippi," and he received a promotion to brigadier general in March 1865; Hardeman went to Mexico after the war, but returned to Texas a few years later; served successively as assistant sergeant-at-arms of the Texas House of Representatives, state inspector of railroads, and superintendent of public buildings and grounds in Austin, which included supervising the Texas Confederate Soldiers' Home. He died in Austin in 1898.

escaped; therefore Wharton took personal command. Skirmishing began at daylight. Parsons recalled that his whole brigade, under Steele, received orders to begin the attack. Other Texas units, including Hamilton P. Bee's Division, consisting of the brigades of Xavier B. Debray and Arthur P. Bagby, as well as James P. Major's Division, including the brigades of William P. Hardeman and George W. Baylor, supported their advance. By 11 A.M. they were joined by Robert Stone's Brigade from Camille Polignac's Infantry Division. A member of Polignac's command recalled that the Texans' "position was a strong one though in an open field. We had the advantage of a large ditch with others to fall back on. We remained here, for half an hour, our artillery just in front shelling (just in front of this field. The woods extended to the Bayou covered with thick undergrowth.)" The mounted troopers of the 19th and 21st regiments were instructed to charge and feel the enemy, while the 12th Texas dismounted to support the movement. As the Federals advanced in force, the 12th occupied a fence-and-hedge line along the side of Norwood's Plantation, where Parsons had ordered the construction of rail breastworks. Hardeman's Brigade, also dismounted, was to the right of the 12th Texas.

Although the 12th fought as infantry, the other regiments of Parsons' Brigade acted as cavalry throughout the day, the 19th as a reserve and a support to artillery under heavy fire on the right. The 21st Texas and one squadron of the battalion rode to the extreme right where the troopers helped brace the line of infantry and dismounted troops. Colonel James E. Harrison remembered: "When Genl Wharton ordered our line forward, we formed in another ditch two hundred yds in front of our first position, still a good one." After a furious cannonade, in which the Confederate artillery silenced the Federal fire, Wharton ordered the line of dismounted cavalry to charge. On the Federal side Mower sent for his reserves, essentially Shaw's Brigade, and ordered the 3rd Indiana Artillery "double-

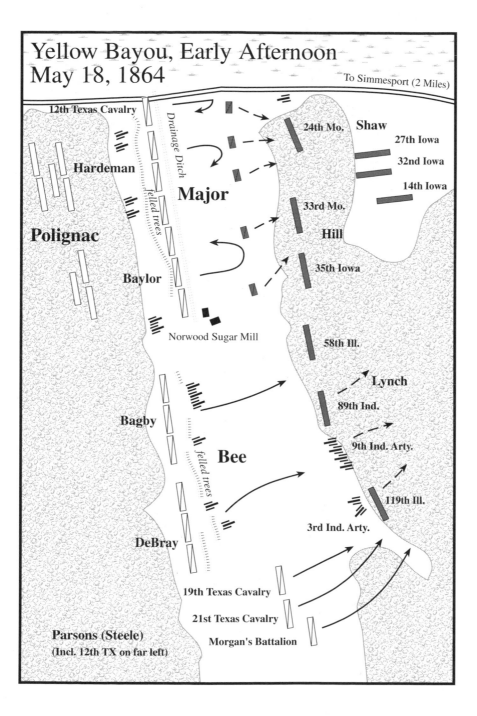

Yellow Bayou, Early Afternoon
May 18, 1864

To Simmesport (2 Miles)

12th Texas Cavalry

Drainage Ditch

felled trees

24th Mo.

Shaw

27th Iowa

32nd Iowa

14th Iowa

Hardeman

Major

33rd Mo.

Polignac

Hill

Baylor

35th Iowa

Norwood Sugar Mill

58th Ill.

Lynch

89th Ind.

Bagby

9th Ind. Arty.

Bee

119th Ill.

3rd Ind. Arty.

felled trees

DeBray

19th Texas Cavalry

21st Texas Cavalry

Parsons (Steele)
(Incl. 12th TX on far left)

Morgan's Battalion

shotted with canister."

After watching the fighting all morning, Colonel Parsons sent word to his superior that an attack would result in great loss of life. Wharton, who expected his orders carried out without protest, became annoyed and issued terse instructions to Harper Goodloe, Parsons' aide-de-camp: "Tell Parsons to charge the enemy at once, or I will prefer charges for disobeying orders." Parsons, whose popularity partially stemmed from his concern for his men, recognized that the odds were heavily on the Union side. Goodloe recalled: "General Parsons was a brave, fearless officer; but as Banks was retreating as rapidly as possible, he wanted to save his men." He refused to order a charge until directed a second time, when he acquiesced, saying, "If I must, I must."

Texans knew how to charge, but were more proficient on horseback than on foot. As the dismounted cavalry moved forward, the Federals strengthened their right and the 12th Texas, positioned on the extreme left, marched straight into a "storm of grape and minnie balls" that decimated the ranks. Yet, Parsons noted, "the line advanced as steadily as infantry veterans over an open field," took position, and "held it until ordered to retire." At a critical moment support came from Captain M.V. McMahan's Galveston Battery. Parsons' horse was wounded, his clothing torn as bullets flew around him. Private Robert Frazier wrote his mother that grape shot and artillery shells fell at times as "thick as hale." At one point the Confederates became confused and began falling back until Colonel Parsons' loud voice shouted: "Halt! What! the gallant 12th behave this way with Federal cavalry on their heels? Halt! and if they charge you wheel and empty their saddles, G__ d__ them." A member of the regiment recalled: "The line was right dressed, and moved out beautifully."

Harper Goodloe recalled: "The charge was ordered through an open field. Our men dismounted and charged the intrenched

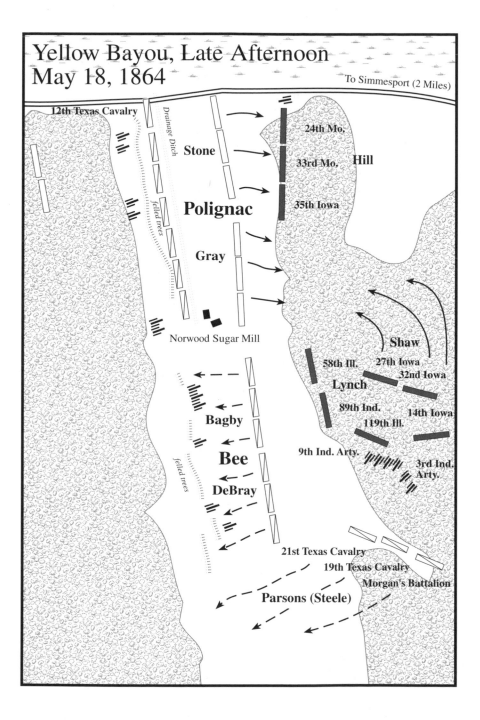

Yellow Bayou, Late Afternoon
May 18, 1864

To Simmesport (2 Miles)

12th Texas Cavalry

Drainage Ditch

felled trees

Stone

24th Mo.

33rd Mo.

Hill

35th Iowa

Polignac

Gray

Norwood Sugar Mill

Shaw

58th Ill.

27th Iowa

32nd Iowa

Lynch

89th Ind.

14th Iowa

119th Ill.

Bagby

9th Ind. Arty.

3rd Ind. Arty.

Bee

felled trees

DeBray

21st Texas Cavalry

19th Texas Cavalry

Morgan's Battalion

Parsons (Steele)

position. A drain ditch across the field a hundred yards in front saved our boys from annihilation, as they got in the ditch and our artillery in the rear opened with shot and shell. The loss in killed and dying from the effects of wounds in the two brigades was over five hundred in a ten-minute charge."

As the Confederates raced for some woods, the 21st Texas and a battalion under Lieutenant Colonel Dewitt Clinton Giddings rode forward. Polignac's brigades also joined in the attack against the Union right center and right flank. Colonel Harrison of the 15th Texas Infantry, Polignac's Division, described the events as he saw them:

> When Genl Wharton ordered us forward to the woods, The La Brigade on the right...moved off by the right flank leaving a wide gap between them and the Texas Brigade, two Regts of which was held in reserve (17th Consolidated and Hawpe's [31st Texas]). [Lieutenant Colonel John H.] Caudle [with the 34th Texas] occupied the left near the levee, I with the 15th Texas o[c]cupied the center, Stone's Battalion [the 22nd Texas] the right. We advanced to the Edge of the field, the fence having been burned away. He[re] we were halted, in ten paces of a wall of thick undergrowth. I rode to Col Stone Comdg Brigade and asked him where he wanted my line formed. He seemed to be at a loss. I told him we had better fall Back to [the] deep ditch one hundred fifty yds to the rear of us, throw out Skirmishers and feel for the Enemy. I believed them to be concealed just before us. He did not fall back but sent out Skirmishers. Th[e]y had not advanced more than sixty steps before they were in ten feet of the 16th Army Corps, rising up in four lines and demanding their surrender. Some of them escaped and got Back, when the four lines were precipitated upon us, and the fight became desperate. Col Caudle's left did not reach the Levee, by one hundred yds, and

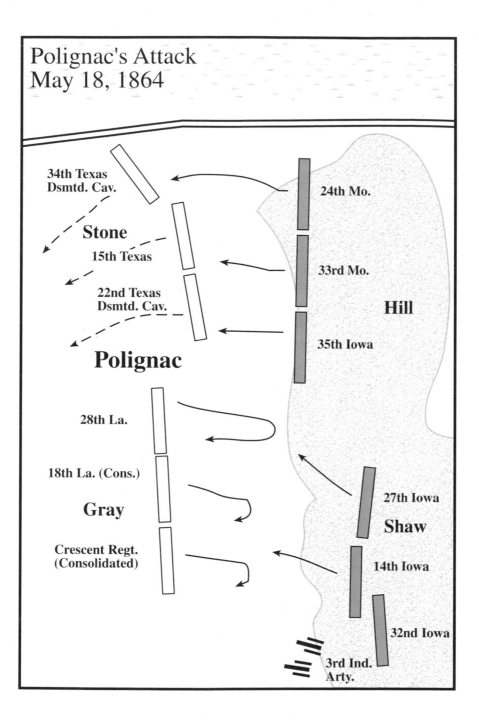

Polignac's Attack
May 18, 1864

34th Texas
Dsmtd. Cav.

24th Mo.

Stone

15th Texas

33rd Mo.

22nd Texas
Dsmtd. Cav.

Hill

35th Iowa

Polignac

28th La.

18th La. (Cons.)

27th Iowa

Gray

Shaw

Crescent Regt.
(Consolidated)

14th Iowa

32nd Iowa

3rd Ind.
Arty.

between the high levee and the Bayou there was a
space of 40 yds, protected by the levee.

Harrison's 15th Texas fought hard as the men of the 34th
Texas began to give ground on their left. "The Ene[m]y moved
a flanking column up the Bayou," recalled Harrison. "Caudle
was soon overwhelmed, and was ordered to fall Back by Col.
Stone. I received no orders, and was engaging four lines to my
front at a distance of 25 and thirty paces. Th[e]y constantly
demanding my surrender. I replied with Enfield Rifles, holding
them steady. [We] cut down their flag Bearers twice, [but]
Th[e]y were promptly raised, and the demand repeated
surrender you damned Rebels or we'l[l] kill you all."

The 15th Texas soon found itself caught in an enfilading fire
between the 34th Texas and the Union flanking column. Some
Rebel cavalrymen, seeing the predicament, dismounted and
pushed the Federals back, allowing the Texans to escape, but
not before Colonel Stone was killed while reporting to
Wharton. Parsons stated that the men with Giddings continued
the fight after the left and center of Polignac's column had
retreated.

As the fighting continued into the afternoon, men on both
sides fell out from exhaustion exacerbated by the intense heat
and humidity. When the Rebel line fell back, the Federals
moved forward and occupied the defenses the Confederates
had hastily constructed. Nature, however, intervened to
hamper the Federals. Colonel Thomas J. Kinney of the 119th
Illinois Infantry, in command of a brigade at Yellow Bayou,
noted the day became "excessively warm, and many of our
men fell from sunstroke and exhaustion. There being no water
in our reach, the men suffered exceedingly for want of it."
Confederate Private Henry Orr wrote his father: "By the time
the boys run back they were so completely exhausted that
some of them fainted." Furthermore, the firing set the
undergrowth ablaze, and smoke and flames obstructed
movements. A.J. Smith later reported: "The firing during the

second charge set the thicket on fire, so that it formed a barrier impassable for either party." Slowly the Southerners fell back to the cover of the bushes, and, when dusk came, the bloodied line retreated.

Although the Texans had cheerfully followed Parsons on foot at Blair's Landing, many questioned the wisdom of this particular attack. Some of the men considered the assault a mistake. Private Orr noted that Wharton was "considerably censured for the manner in which he managed the fight." Colonel Xavier Debray of the 26th Texas Cavalry observed that the whole mess created an "unfortunate and unnecessary affair, the only result of which was to delay the enemy in reaching the eastern side of the Atchafalaya [River], where we wanted him to go, [and it] cost us over two hundred men killed and wounded." But perhaps an officer in the 21st Texas had a simpler explanation when he wrote: "This was one of the bloodiest battles fought West of the Mississippi River—in which we got decently licked. The battle continued about six hours and was fiercely fought on both sides and there was great slaughter to both—I did not think that battle ought to have been fought."

Indeed, losses were significant. Taylor claimed around 452 killed and wounded and 156 taken prisoner, while the Federals reported 38 killed, 226 wounded, and three missing. Parsons' Brigade squandered more in this one charge than in any other battle in the war. An incomplete listing reported twelve killed, sixty-seven wounded, and two missing. Of this number, the 12th Texas lost ten killed, sixty-one wounded, and two missing.

But Parsons' Texans had a reputation to uphold, and they wanted to ensure that Banks did indeed abandon central Louisiana. Certainly, if truth be told, by 1864 Parsons' Texans had lost the enthusiasm for the war that had sustained them throughout the early years. But they still assaulted with as much determination as they had in their initial battle in 1862, when they attacked full of self-confidence and high expectations. Even Federal troops recognized the intensity of their purpose. A Union soldier recalled how the Rebels had attacked again and again "with a stubbornness and impetuosity" that reminded him "of the sort of assault Nathan Beford Forrest was accustomed to make." This, concluded historian Ludwell Johnson, was "high praise indeed." Colonel Thomas J. Kinney of the 119th Illinois Infantry believed that Yellow Bayou was "one of the most severe battles of the war."

The Confederates, however, could justly brag that they had prevented an invasion of Texas. The political decision allowing Banks to go up the Red River instead of against Mobile may have had widespread military implications well beyond the expedition itself. "Had Banks' forces been moving eastward against Mobile rather than westward toward Texas, " speculated historian Richard McMurry, "it seems highly unlikely that the Confederate Government would have dared to send [Leonidas] Polk's Army of Mississippi and some of the garrison troops from Mobile and Florida to reinforce [Joseph E.] Johnston's army in Georgia." If Polk's 20,000 men had not joined the Army of Tennessee, and if Sherman had not loaned 10,000 men to Banks, the Union Army might have moved on Atlanta more rapidly.

Whatever the results, Parsons' horsemen had been part of the little army that pushed Banks down the Red River. During the campaign, they fought the only way they knew. The colonel had not learned his military skill from a textbook; he had absorbed military tactics from his Mexican War service and taught his men the art of frontal assault. During the Civil War he repeatedly utilized the mounted charge successfully, although sabers and shotguns were sometimes discarded in favor of the new repeating carbines when possible. Other than at Yellow Bayou, however, Parsons' men never had the opportunity to launch a large-scale attack; their cavalry charges in the past usually involved small groups—companies or squadrons against companies or squadrons of equal size.

Moreover, they seldom fought dismounted and, as cavalry, they had never faced an army; therefore, before Yellow Bayou, Parsons' troopers had not needed a complicated plan of battle. What they knew best was a simple broad attack on the enemy's front. Parsons' Texans had built a well-deserved reputation upon their dashing attacks, and a certain amount of peer pressure sustained this distinction. If these Texans used the charge over and over again, it was because it was an uncomplicated method of engaging the enemy—and it worked. There was no practicality in rejecting a tactic that never failed them, at least until Yellow Bayou. Most of the casualties sustained in the Red River Campaign came at Yellow Bayou when the troops fought on foot. Because they were not experienced in this kind of fighting, Parsons lost more men in this one battle than in any other in the war.

Nevertheless, the rough reception the Confederates provided the invading Union army guaranteed Banks' continued flight down the Red River. Perhaps the best compliment to the Southern defenders came from young Kate Stone, a Louisiana refugee living in East Texas. Kate, whose home was a large cotton plantation in northeast Louisiana, about thirty miles northwest of Vicksburg, Mississippi, observed from her temporary lodgings in Tyler: "We will never laugh at our soldiers on this side of the Mississippi again."

7

CONFEDERATE CAVALRY AND THE TEXAS FRONTIER TRADITION

Through the war Southern cavalry had to abide constant criticism, not only from the enlisted foot soldier but also from those in positions of power. One Confederate general complained: "It often appeared to me that many of our failures or misfortunes arose from our lamentable deficiency in this branch of the service." Another Southerner, believing the undisciplined cavalry a judgment on the South, told his wife, "It seems that a just Providence still thinks we have not suffered enough." A high-ranking Confederate, trying to determine how many men were in one Western army, listed only infantry and artillery, and explained: "I dont count Cavalry ...though it is an admirable arm of the service to get up sensational paragraphs." A Texan with the Army of Tennessee observed: "A distinguished lieutenant general is reported as saying that [the 8th Texas Cavalry] was not a regiment at all, but 'd__ d armed mob.' If there was ever any serious attempt to discipline it the effort was soon abandoned. Volunteers we began, volunteers we remained to the end. If any wished to evade duty, they found a way, and the punishment for evasion was light. To our credit it may be said that few ever avoided a fight."

The informality in the units created a unique bond between the men and their commanders, and often meant troopers proved reluctant to take orders from an outsider, particularly if they considered the order foolish. Trans-Mississippi cavalry seemed to have a more pragmatic outlook on military matters, possibly because their primary duties of scouting and raiding afforded them almost total freedom of movement. Most commanders in the department resigned themselves to the near impossibility of making disciplined soldiers out of the Texans.

Disciplined or not, Texas cavalry remained busy in two theaters of war during the spring of 1864. When Sherman began his movement toward Atlanta, Joseph E. Johnston had only two Texas cavalry regiments, the 8th and the 11th, but these Texas Rangers had earned a reputation that far exceeded their small number. During the Atlanta Campaign the four regiments in Ross' Texas Cavalry brigade joined them. These six regiments, under the command of Joseph Wheeler, skirmished with Sherman's cavalry throughout the campaign, occasionally fighting dismounted. When John Bell Hood left Georgia with the Army of Tennessee, he took Ross' Brigade with him, and those Texans participated in the disastrous battles in Tennessee. Most of the 8th and 11th Texas stayed with Wheeler, and became part of the small cavalry force that badgered Sherman on his March to the Sea. Because of their involvement in some of the most celebrated battles in the Western theater, the men in these six regiments were probably the best known of all Texas cavalrymen.

Nevertheless, while these six regiments gained fame in Georgia and Tennessee, other Texas cavalry units had participated in halting Banks' Red River Campaign, and another force of mounted Texans took part in the campaign in Arkansas. But because these units were in the Trans-Mississippi Department, the men never received the accolades of their counterparts who fought with the Army of Tennessee.

Although Texas cavalry could fight dismounted, as they did during the Red River Campaign, they rarely distinguished themselves when separated from their horses. In fact, it is safe to say that most Texas cavalrymen generally made poor infantry. Perhaps John Bell Hood, who criticized the use of dismounted cavalry, was correct when he said: "A cavalryman...cannot be trained to fight, one day, mounted, the next, dismounted, and then be expected to charge with the impetuosity of one who has been educated in the belief that it is an easy matter to ride over infantry and artillery, and drive them from the field. He who fights alternately mounted and dismounted, can never become an excellent soldier of either infantry or cavalry."

By 1864 cavalry tactics were changing, and Texans were not strangers to the revolutionary innovations. Although some cavalry leaders still preferred to take the offensive by charging, this became rare as the realities of new weaponry made it increasingly impractical. Nevertheless, Texans were often reluctant to give up their shotguns, six-shooters, and Bowie knives; these weapons were a mark of distinction that declared the bearer a Texan. This formed a part of the Texas mystique. The Texas Revolution, the Alamo, San Jacinto—these were events of legendary magnitude by the time of the Civil War, for a quarter of a century had passed since Texans had won their independence from Mexico.

As traditional uses for cavalry became obsolete in the face

of increased firepower, however, Texans, like other Confederate cavalry, finally traded in their obsolete weapons for modern ones whenever possible. With the increased use of breechloaders, cavalry was often utilized as mounted infantry. In fact, resourceful cavalry leaders such as Forrest dismounted his men more and more often.

But the Texans had not joined the army to fight on foot, and the exhilaration that came from attacking on horseback often overpowered a man's sense of reason. Rather than becoming more careful toward the end of the war, Texans frequently became more reckless. After a lively skirmish between the Texans under Joseph Wheeler and Sherman' cavalry in southeast Georgia, a Federal major wrote: "A cavalry fight is just about as much fun as a fox hunt; but, of course, in the midst of the fun somebody is getting hurt all the time."

Nevertheless, even after they knew the cause was lost, Texans did not lose their determination to fight, nor did they become more cautious. At the Battle of Bentonville, North Carolina, on March 21, 1865, about eighty Texans formed part of a small force that charged Sherman's veteran Seventeenth Corps, temporarily driving the Federal soldiers back. Perhaps the most notable event of this mounted charge, probably one of the last that Texans made in the Civil War, was the death of Lieutenant General William J. Hardee's son. The boy had run away from school in Georgia to join the famed Texas Rangers, only to be returned to the classroom by his exasperated father. But after a second escape, the teenager had persuaded his father to allow him to join the Texans, and this was his first battle. Joseph E. Johnston reported that General Hardee's son, "a very promising youth of sixteen, fell mortally wounded when gallantly charging in the foremost ranks [of the Texans]."

Even as defeat and surrender claimed the Southern armies, Texas cavalrymen remained intolerant of discipline. During the truce between Johnston and Sherman in April 1865, Wheeler

**In February 1865 Union cavalry commander Judson Kilpatrick charged:
"An infantry lieutenant and seven men were murdered yesterday by the
Eighth Texas Cavalry after they had surrendered. We found their bodies all
together and mutilated, with paper on their breasts, saying, 'Death to
foragers.' Eighteen of my men were killed yesterday and some had**

their throats cut." Whether or not the Texans were responsible, the
men from the 8th Texas Cavalry (Terry's Texas Rangers) such as those
pictured here, had acquired enough of a reputation that Kilpatrick
singled them out for retaliation.

complained: "I have succeeded in getting most of the men back to their commands, except those from the Eighth Texas. There are only seventy-eight of that regiment now in camp. I have parties now out after those still absent, and hope to secure the return of most of them."

Where had the Texans gone? One member of the regiment recalled that the officers "allowed all men who wished, without being paroled, to leave. The intention was to join Kirby Smith" and continue the fight on the west side of the Mississippi. Another Texan recalled that "about one hundred and fifty of us started home, without permission or parole. We rode out of the army lines at night—we had a lieutenant as commander." In mid-January 1865 there had been nearly 550 Texans with the 8th Texas; at the surrender, one veteran insisted there were only 175.

Those who left were headed home to fight for Texas. All through the war Texas cavalrymen had been proud of their distinctiveness, and quick to remind everyone that they were Confederates, but Confederates from the Lone Star State. Texas had no celebrated cavalry units like Jeb Stuart's or Phil Sheridan's, and few men of national fame. The only full general Texas produced, Albert Sidney Johnston, died at Shiloh; Hood, who claimed Texas as his home, is not always claimed by Texans. Although Kirby Smith made some promotions these were never officially confirmed by Richmond. Only two Texans appointed major general actually received approval from Jefferson Davis. Both commanded cavalry. The first, Thomas Lafayette Rosser, major general of cavalry in Virginia, spent his teenage years in Texas, but did not return after the war. He did, however, go on to become one of three former Confederates to serve in the Spanish-American War. Because of Rosser's defection from Texas, he is generally considered a Virginian, and he died in Charlottesville, Virginia, in 1910. John Austin Wharton, the second of the two, would have been a native Texan had his mother not been visiting Tennessee when he was born. He died before the war ended, April 6, 1865, after being shot in a Houston hotel by fellow Texan, Colonel George W. Baylor, following a private argument between the two.

The great majority of the Texans who served in the Confederate cavalry were ordinary men whose names never made it into the history books. They were mainly farmers who knew how to protect their homes from the Indians and could fire a gun at a gallop. They knew little about military tactics, and abhorred military discipline. They proved excellent soldiers when mounted, but not as effective when separated from their horses. Often they did what came naturally, and would have been surprised to learn that they were using some of the tactics suggested by Joseph Wheeler in his popular manual for Southern cavalrymen. Few of them had read any books on military tactics; indeed, some could not even read. But they fought in a way that came naturally, fired by a courage and a conviction to protect a cause they considered just. One veteran summed up why Texas cavalry was so successful. "The men were all good horsemen," he explained, "accustomed to the use and management of horses from childhood. When three or four hundred of such men, charging as fast as their horses would go, yelling like Comanches, each delivering twelve shots with great rapidity and reasonable accuracy, burst into the ranks of an enemy, the enemy generally gave way. It did not take us long to find this out; [unfortunately] also the enemy were not slow to 'catch on' [either]."

There was nothing glamorous about being a Texas cavalryman, and few of these men would be remembered. When operating as scouts and raiders, they moved continually regardless of the weather, and slept on the ground wherever they stopped. They seldom had the luxury of a tent, often bedding down in mud or snow. They foraged for food, not only for themselves, but for their horses, and both man and beast often went hungry. Continued exposure to the elements meant that sickness took a heavy toll, and desertion was not unknown. Toward the end of the war many units were forced to dismount as horses and forage simply gave out. It is true that battle deaths were fewer in the cavalry, but privation and hardship remained the men's constant companions. In spite of justifiable complaints about the often undisciplined and troublesome cavalry, the Texas troopers constituted a vital arm of the Confederate army, and played an important, but often overlooked, role in the war in the West.

FURTHER READING

Anderson, John Q., ed. *Brokenburn: The Journal of Kate Stone, 1861–1868*; Baton Rouge: Louisiana State University Press, 1955, 1972.

_____. *Campaigning with Parsons' Texas Cavalry Brigade, CSA: The War Journals and Letters of the Four Orr Brothers, 12th Texas Cavalry Regiment.* Hillsboro, Texas: Hill Junior College Press, 1967.

Bailey, Anne J. *Between the Enemy and Texas: Parsons's Texas Cavalry in the Civil War.* Fort Worth: Texas Christian University Press, 1987.

Barr, Alwyn. *Polignac's Texas Brigade.* Houston: Texas Gulf Coast Historical Association, 1964.

Barron, Samuel B. *The Lone Star Defenders: A Chronicle of the Third Texas Cavalry Regiment in the Civil War.* 1908; reprint, Washington, D.C.: Zenger Publishing Co., 1983.

Blessington, J. P. *The Campaigns of Walker's Texas Division.* 1875; reprint, Austin: State House Press, 1994.

Bragg, Jefferson Davis. *Louisiana in the Confederacy.* Baton Rouge: Louisiana State University Press, 1941, 1994.

Brown, Norman E., ed. *Journey to Pleasant Hill: The Civil War Letters of Captain Elijah P. Petty, Walker's Texas Division, C.S.A.* San Antonio: Institute of Texan Cultures, 1982.

Cater, Douglas John. *As It Was: Reminiscences of a Soldier of the Third Texas Cavalry and the Nineteenth Louisiana Infantry.* 1981; reprint, Austin: State House Press, 1990.

Christ, Mark K., ed. *Rugged and Sublime: The Civil War in Arkansas.* Fayetteville: University of Arkansas Press, 1994.

Cutrer, Thomas W. *Ben McCulloch and the Frontier Military Tradition.* Chapel Hill: University of North Carolina Press, 1993.

DeBray, Xavier, F. *A Sketch of the History of DeBray's Twenty-Sixth Regiment of Texas Cavalry.* Austin: E. Von Boeckman, 1884.

Faulk, Okie B. *General Tom Green: Fightin' Texan.* Waco: Texian Press, 1963.

Ford, John Salmon. *Rip Ford's Texas.* Edited by Stephen B. Oates. Austin: University of Texas Press, 1968.

Gallaway, B.P. *The Ragged Rebel: A Common Soldier in W.H. Parsons' Texas Cavalry, 1861–1865.* Austin: University of Texas Press, 1988.

Garrett, David R. *The Civil War Letters of David R. Garrett, Detailing the Adventures of the 6th Texas Cavalry,* 1861-1865. Edited by Max S. Lale and Hobart Key, Jr. Marshall, Texas, 1967.

Giles, L.B. *Terry's Texas Rangers.* 1911; reprint, Austin: The Pemberton Press, 1967.

Graber, H.W. *A Terry Texas Ranger: The Life Record of H.W. Graber.* 1916; reprint, Austin: State House Press, 1987.

Griscom, George L. *Fighting with Ross' Texas Cavalry Brigade: The Diary of George L. Griscom, Adjutant, 9th Texas Cavalry Regiment.* Edited by Homer L. Kerr. Hillsboro, Texas: Hill Junior College Press, 1976.

Hale, Douglas. *The Third Texas Cavalry in the Civil War.* Norman: University of Oklahoma Press, 1993.

Heartsill, W.W. *Fourteen Hundred and 91 Days in the Confederate Army.* Edited by Bell Irvin Wiley. 1876; reprints, 1954; Wilmington, N.C.: Broadfoot Publishing Co., 1992.

Jeffries, C.C. *Terry's Rangers.* New York: Vantage Press, 1961.

Johnson, Ludwell H. *Red River Campaign: Politics and Cotton in the Civil War.* 1958; reprint, Kent, Ohio: Kent State University Press, 1993.

Kerby, Robert L. *Kirby Smith's Confederacy: The Trans-Mississippi South, 1863–1865.* 1972; reprint, Tuscaloosa and London: University of Alabama Press, 1991.

Lubbock, Francis R. *Six Decades in Texas: The Memoirs of Francis Richard Lubbock, Governor of Texas in War-Time, 1861–1863.* Edited by C. W. Raines. 1900; reprint, Austin: The Pemberton Press, 1968.

Neal, Diane and Thomas W. Kremm. *The Lion of the South: General Thomas C. Hindman.* Macon: Mercer University Press, 1993.

Nunn, W.C. *Ten More Texans in Gray.* Hillsboro, Texas: Hill Junior College Press, 1980.

_____. *Ten Texans in Gray*. Hillsboro, Texas: Hill Junior College Press, 1968.

Oates, Stephen B. *Confederate Cavalry West of the River*. 1961; reprint, Austin: University of Texas Press, 1992.

Parks, Joseph Howard. *General Edmund Kirby Smith, C.S.A.* Baton Rouge: Louisiana State University Press, 1954.

Parrish, T. Michael. *Richard Taylor: Soldier Prince of Dixie*. Chapel Hill: University of North Carolina Press, 1992.

Rose, Victor M. *Ross' Texas Brigade: Being a Narrative of Events Connected with its Service in the Late War Between the States*. 1881; reprint, Kennesaw, Georgia: Continental Book Co., 1960.

Smith, David Paul. *Frontier Defense in the Civil War: Texas' Rangers and Rebels*. College Station: Texas A&M University Press, 1992, 1994.

Starr, Stephen Z. *The Union Cavalry in the Civil War*. vol. 3: *The War in the West 1861–1865*. Baton Rouge: Louisiana State University Press, 1985.

Taylor, Richard. *Destruction and Reconstruction: Personal Experiences of the Late War*. 1879; reprints, 1968; Time-Life Books, 1983.

Terrell, Alexander Watkins. *From Texas to Mexico and the Court of Maximilian in 1865*. Dallas: The Book Club of Texas, 1933.

Walton, William M. (Buck). *An Epitome of My Life: Civil War Reminiscences*. Austin: The Waterloo Press, 1965.

Winters, John D. *The Civil War in Louisiana*. Baton Rouge: Louisiana State University Press, 1963, 1995.

Wright, Marcus J., comp. *Texas in the War, 1861–1865*. Edited by Harold B. Simpson. Hillsboro, Texas: Hill Junior College Press, 1965.

Yeary, Mamie, compiler. *Reminiscences of the Boys in Gray, 1861–1865*. 1912; reprint, Dayton, Ohio: Morningside House, Inc., 1986.

Zuber, William Physick. *My Eighty Years in Texas*. Edited by Janis Boyle Mayfield. Austin: University of Texas Press, 1971.

PHOTO CREDITS

We thank the Harold B. Simpson Confederate Research Center, Hillsboro, Texas, for permission to reproduce photographs of Nathaniel M. Burford, Edward Clark, Xavier B. Debray, Francis R. Lubbock, James Major, Oran M. Roberts, Benjamin Franklin Terry, and the Parsons' Brigade Battle Flag. We are especially grateful to Mrs. Peggy Fox for her help.

We're grateful to the Unites States Army Military History Institute, Carlisle Barracks, Pennsylvania, for photographs of J.K.P. Blackburn, Willaim P. Hardeman, David D. Porter, Thomas O. Selfridge, Andrew J. Smith, Richard Taylor, and John Austin Wharton.

The source of the picture of the Confederate attack on Admiral David D. Porter's fleet is *Harpers New Monthly Magazine*, April 1865.

The photograph of William Henry Parsons is used through the courtesy of William D. Parsons, Lake Forest, Illinois.

The picture of Sam J. Richardson is used as it appeared in W.W. Heartsill's *Fourteen Hundred and 91 Days in the Confederate Army*, published in 1876.

We acknowledge the Panhandle-Plains Historical Society, Canyon, Texas, for providing the photograph of Terry's Texas Rangers.

For the picture of Thomas Green we credit the Archives Division, Texas State Library, Austin, Texas.

INDEX